CHINESE
COOKING
MADE EASY

COMPILED BY DOUGLAS MARSLAND

TORMONT

CONTENTS

This edition is published with the permission of
HarperCollins Publishers Pty Limited.

Published in 1993 by
Tormont Publications Inc.
338 Saint Antoine St. East
Montreal, Canada H2Y 1A3
Tel. (514) 954-1441
Fax (514) 954-1443
ISBN 2-89429-391-7
Printed in Canada

Copyright © Bay Books

Cover photograph by Ashley Mackevicius and styled by Wendy Berecry

DISCOVER THE DELIGHTS OF
CHINESE CUISINE

Discover the delights of Chinese cuisine with food that's easy to prepare and cook. Chinese cooking is famous for its variety, its subtle tastes, and its beautifully built-in balance of foods.

Chinese cooking is one of the world's great cuisines, popular in many countries around the world. Superb combinations of flavors and textures also offer the bonus of good health. It has been described as the ideal diet for our modern times, being high in protein and complex carbohydrates and low in fat and calories. It also caters to vegetarians and people on a low cholesterol diet. Meat plays a secondary role and vegetables, particularly the non-starchy varieties, predominate.

Grains are plentiful, mainly rice and wheat. Rice is grown in the south and forms the staple diet. It is also used for noodle making and flour. Wheat is grown in the north and north-west, and used for flour and many varieties of noodles, which are served in place of rice.

Meats used are low in fat and other high protein foods play an important role. For hundreds of years soybeans have been used for their rich protein, which closely resembles that of meat. Soybeans often are ground and mixed with water, converting them into a milky substance, then into a curd which is pressed into blocks called bean curd or tofu.

Bean curd can be dried, deep-fried, salted, made into sauces, steamed or eaten fresh. Soybean sprouts are also eaten as a vegetable.

Sweets are seldom eaten. The Chinese prefer savory foods. Between-meal snacks include many delicious dumplings, steamed buns and dim sum. Fresh fruit is usually served at the end of a family meal. The few dessert recipes that exist are usually reserved for banquets.

The format of a family meal is simple. Every dish is served on the table at the same time, not in courses as in the West.

Most modern food markets have pork, chicken and beef shredded or cut into chunks, as well as a variety of marinated meats and poultry. Chinese food stores sell freshly roasted and barbecued pork and cooked ducks and chickens, whole and in portions. These are easily kept on hand for quick meals by slicing, dicing and freezing in recipe-size quantities.

Many ingredients, such as water chestnuts and lychees, are available in cans, and a great variety of ready-made sauces can be found on the shelves of most supermarkets and Asian food stores.

CHINESE COOKING CLASS

Chinese cooking is easy when you know how. In the following pages, we look at cooking utensils and how to use them, and the basic methods of cooking Chinese-style. The rest is a little practice, a little experimenting, and lots of visits to Chinese restaurants to compare results.

1 *Wok*
2 *Ladle*
3 *Wok rack*
4 *Steamer*
5 *Chopping board*
6 *Cleaver*
7 *Clay pot*
8 *Wire-mesh strainer*
9 *Spatula*

BASIC KITCHEN UTENSILS

We all have our own favorite knives, pots and pans for cooking, and these can be used with great success for Chinese cooking. In a Chinese kitchen, the utensils are very few but practical, namely the wok, bamboo steamers, cleavers, spatulas, strainers and chopsticks.

The wok is a thin metal all-purpose cooking pan, with high sides and rounded bottom. It can be used for stir-frying, deep-frying, par-boiling, simmering, braising, boiling and steaming. By placing a set of steaming baskets into the wok, a first-class steamer is made, which will enable as many as five different dishes to be cooked at the same time e.g. fish, dim sum, egg rolls, chicken or duck, and rice. The wok is also ideal for omelets and for outdoor cooking.

The wok spatula is designed to fit the curvature of the wok. It is used mainly for stir-fry dishes, to turn food and prevent burning or sticking.

Light and heavy cleavers are both made from tempered steel; the light cleaver is used for slicing meat and vegetables and the heavy cleaver is used for chopping through bones, crab and lobster shells. The opposing edge is used for mashing and when held upright, the handle serves as a grinder for spices and black beans.

The flat sides of the cleaver are used for transferring chopped food from the board to serving plates, pounding and tenderizing meats, crushing ginger and garlic and, when combined with the light cleaver, forms an excellent mincer.

Wire-mesh strainers are used for removing deep-fried foods from hot oil, draining off excess oil and in the making of potato and noodle baskets.

Chopsticks come in various sizes, with an extra long size to be used in the kitchen for beating eggs, adding and removing food from a deep-fryer, turning food while cooking, adding beaten egg to soups, and removing ingredients from jars.

Optional extras include *steam boats* for Mongolian hot pot, small *cooking baskets* for steam boat cookery and a *tong hock* for measuring and transferring liquids.

CHINESE METHODS OF COOKING

The main styles of cooking are: stir-frying, steaming, deep-frying and roasting, all with a minimum of fuel, which in former days was a matter of necessity. In early days, wood, coal and charcoal were used. Today all these forms of cooking are carried out with modern gas and electric ranges, electric woks and microwave ovens, still with consideration towards economy.

STIR-FRYING This technique is used for tender cuts of pork and beef, poultry, seafood and vegetables. The ingredients are sliced, shredded, diced or minced, then stir-fried in a wok using a spatula. Cook over high heat with a minimum of oil. This method seals in the natural juices and preserves color, texture and flavor.

Gas is preferred for Chinese cooking for the instant control of temperature. If using an electric stove, flat-bottomed woks are available from most Chinese food stores.

Ingredients are added to the wok in order of texture and cooking time. The preparation of ingredients and being well-organized are the keys to success in Chinese cooking:

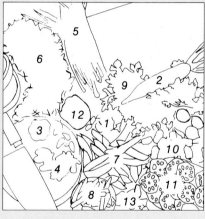

1	*Dried mushrooms*	**8**	*Baby or mini corn*
2	*White radish*	**9**	*Fresh coriander*
3	*Garlic*	**10**	*Chili peppers*
4	*Fresh ginger*	**11**	*Lotus root*
5	*Green onions*	**12**	*Red pepper*
6	*Bean sprouts*	**13**	*Dried tangerine peel*
7	*Snow peas*		

❖ Collect all ingredients required for the recipe. Allow time for soaking dried ingredients like Chinese mushrooms.

❖ Slice meat, poultry and seafood. Arrange in order of cooking on a large platter. Prepare marinades if required, and marinate. This can take up to 30 minutes.

❖ Wash, drain and cut vegetables to size. Parboil or blanch if necessary.

❖ Measure liquid ingredients like oil, sauces, stock and seasonings. Blend any thickening agent with stock or water and stir before adding to wok. Chop ginger, garlic and chili peppers. Arrange ingredients in the order that they will be added to the wok for cooking.

❖ Collect cooking utensils and warm serving dishes.

This basic preparation should be done for all recipes before any style

Stir-frying: prepare vegetables in advance.

Heat oil in a wok until very hot. Fry garlic and ginger first to flavor oil.

Add larger, denser vegetables and pour in sauce or stock.

of Chinese cooking is started as it makes Chinese cooking easy. Confucius once said, "Cooked Chinese food waits not for any man". It should be served and eaten at once, to experience the best flavor, texture and color of the food.

DEEP-FRYING The deep-frying technique is used extensively throughout Chinese cuisine, from hors d'oeuvres to main course dishes and desserts. You can use a great variety of ingredients, such as pork, beef, poultry, seafood, vegetables, various types of noodles, and fruit.

Deep-frying ingredients are cut into even-sized pieces and dipped into a protective coating of batter, such as seasoned flour, beaten egg and breadcrumbs, or spring roll or wonton wrappers. Then they are immersed in hot oil to cover, until cooked.

Oil or shortening should be heated to 350°F (180°C) in a deep-fryer or deep-sided saucepan, not more than half full.

If a saucepan is used without a thermometer, a slice of fresh ginger can be added to indicate the oil's temperature. When the ginger turns golden, the oil is right for deep-frying.

On reaching 350°F (180°C) oil or shortening will cease to bubble, and a faint blue haze will start to rise.

Tips for optimum deep-frying results include:

❖ Marinated ingredients should be drained before dipping into batter and being fried.

❖ Ingredients can be two-thirds cooked, then drained. Just prior to serving, oil can be reheated to the correct temperature, and the final stage of deep-frying completed. This gives even cooking and a crisp texture. This method is called double-frying.

❖ Only add small quantities of ingredients to the oil at one time. This maintains the oil's temperature and prevents excess oil absorption.

❖ Drain food thoroughly and serve with prepared dips or sauces.

❖ Allow oil to cool then strain. Store covered to prevent dust from settling on the surface.

Add a quantity of fresh oil to used oil before re-using; this prevents oil from discoloring and gives a higher smoke point when reheating.

ROASTING Roasting in China originally took place outdoors on large spits or from hanging hooks over open fires.

The Chinese style of roasting can be done in the modern oven by making wire hooks and hanging, from the top shelf of the oven, marinated duck, chicken or strips of pork brushed with barbecue sauce, with a roasting dish containing an inch or so (several centimeters) of water placed underneath to catch the drips.

Roasting can also be done by placing a cake rack over a roasting pan containing 1–2 inches (2–5 cm) of water, and placing the meats onto the rack. Meat should not sit flat in a roasting dish stewing in its own juices as it tends to become tough.

Roasting starts with high heat, which is later reduced to medium. Baste during cooking with marinades or honey and warm water.

STEAMING Cooking by the steaming method enables three to five preparations to be cooked at the same time, with the minimum of fuel. Chinese steaming baskets are made from bamboo and consist of two baskets and a lid. They come in various sizes, and extra baskets can be purchased individually. A new bamboo steamer should be soaked in water overnight before it is used the first time. Chinese metal steamers are also available. They have two baskets with a lid and a pot-style base, and can be used for direct and indirect steaming. The base and lid can serve as a saucepan or be used for stewing long-cooking ingredients.

DIRECT STEAMING Bamboo steamers are placed into a wok containing an inch or so (several centimeters) of vigorously boiling water. Food to be steamed can be placed on a heatproof plate or dish, or on banana leaves cut to basket size, Chinese cabbage or lettuce leaves. Always leave enough room for the steam to circulate around the food and cook it by direct contact. Place a clean cloth over the top basket before putting the lid on. This will absorb condensation and prevent it from dripping onto the steamed products.

A tight-fitting, dome-shaped wok lid is essential for steaming to keep the steam in. The dome shape allows condensation to run down the sides of the lid rather than dripping onto the food.

Steaming time varies with different foods. Dumplings and dim sum take 20 minutes, a whole fish weighing 1½ lbs (675 g) will cook in 15 minutes, while medium-sized chickens and larger cuts of pork take 40 minutes. The longer cooking items are placed in the lower baskets and other baskets are placed on top in order of cooking times.

INDIRECT STEAMING This is usually done in a heatproof bowl, which can be covered with aluminum foil. The bowl is placed in a large saucepan or pot with its ingredients. Boiling water is added to surround the bowl to about half it height. Then the saucepan lid is put on. The water must remain boiling during the cooking time. Check water level during steaming. Extra boiling water should be added if necessary for both methods of steaming.

Food cooked by indirect steaming includes: whole ducks, whole chickens, slow-cooked stewed meats and savory custards. It is also an effective method for reheating rice. Steamed food is best slightly undercooked, as it continues cooking in its own stored heat after being removed from the steamer.

SIMMER COOKING This gentle method of cooking is used for soups and slow cooking of less tender cuts of meat. It is also suitable for seafoods to avoid overcooking. A stock or sauce is brought to a boil with the ingredients added, then simmered over low heat until tender.

PARBOILING is used when cooking ingredients of different textures. The tougher varieties are added to boiling stock or water for a short time. They are then refreshed in iced water to set color and prevent overcooking. When the parboiled foods are cooked with more tender ingredients, the cooking time will then be the same.

CHINESE FIRE POT COOKING The Chinese fire pot is an example of simmer cooking. It enables a larger number of diners to be catered to and to participate in the cooking, which is done at the table.

Fire pots, or steam boats as they are also called, are made from a variety of metals. Individual wire baskets or chopsticks are used to cook the food in small quantities, in simmering stock. Hot coals or heat beads are placed into the chimney in the center of the cooking container. This keeps the stock simmering. An electric frying pan can substitute for the fire pot.

The fire pot is placed in the center of the dining table on a heatproof tray or on a cutting board covered with aluminum foil. Boiling stock is poured into the container, and the raw ingredients and condiments are placed around the pot.

Each diner selects and cooks food, which is then dipped into various sauces or raw egg. Steamed rice and Chinese tea are served with the meal, which can last several hours.

A fire pot or steam boat is used to cook dishes such as Mongolian Hot Pot

GLOSSARY

ABALONE (DRIED, FRESH OR CANNED)
A large mollusc used in soups, stir-fried dishes and salads. Slice fresh abalone thinly. Abalone only needs to be heated through. It will toughen if overheated.

AGAR AGAR A variety of dried seaweed which resembles vermicelli noodles. It must be soaked before use and can be used to replace gelatine. Available dried in powder and stick form.

BAMBOO SHOOTS Young shoots of the bamboo, cut when just appearing above ground. Available in various size cans, whole, sliced or braised. Use as a vegetable or in combination dishes.

BEAN CURD A bland custard-like product made from soybeans, also known as bean cake or tofu. Available fresh, vacuum-packed, canned and dried. The texture can be firm or soft. Firm textured curd is suitable for braising, deep-frying, soups, steaming or stir-frying with other ingredients. Soft-textured curd can be used in various fillings or soups, or eaten fresh with a dip sauce. Bean curd can be blanched then refreshed before eating fresh. The dried form requires soaking in warm water before using in soups or as a wrapper.

BEAN PASTE, SWEET RED Red beans cooked with sugar, then puréed. Available canned in various sizes and used as a filling in steamed pastries and puddings.

BEAN SAUCE A thick sauce made from fermented soybeans. Hot bean sauce contains chili pepper and spices.

BEANS SPROUTS These are the sprouts of mung beans. They sprout within a few days and can be grown at home indoors. The texture is crisp and the taste delicate. They are cooked briefly in stir-fried dishes and used in salads, soups and vegetable combinations. They are readily available fresh or canned.

BEAN SPROUTS, SOY Soybean sprouts are larger than mung bean sprouts and have a slightly stronger flavor. Blanch in boiling water for 1 minute and refresh in cold water, if using in salads. Can be used to replace mung bean sprouts.

BEANS, FERMENTED BLACK These fermented small black beans are strongly flavored. Use in suggested amounts with garlic and ginger in braised dishes, sauces, stir-fried beef, pork, chicken and seafood. Available in cans or jars and dried in packages of various sizes. The dried variety tend to be salty – soak in warm water or sherry before using to reduce the salty flavor. Store in a jar in cupboard after opening, do not refrigerate.

BEANS, YELLOW These fermented soybeans are actually light brown. When mashed, they can be stir-fried with garlic and ginger to form a sauce base for chicken, pork and seafood. They are much milder in flavor than black beans. Ready-made sauce is also available canned.

BIRD'S NESTS These famous ingredients are actually the nests of seaside swallows. Nests are made from small fish, seaweed and marine plants, which the swallow collects and pulls apart then mixes with saliva to form a nest, which is very gelatinous and rich in protein and vitamins. As the nest becomes very dry and hard, it must be soaked and boiled for several hours before using. Three grades are available: the most expensive are the whole nests, then broken nests and last, the small nest fragments. Bird's nest soup is served at formal banquets and is considered a delicacy. All grades are sold by weight.

BITTER MELON (BALSAM PEAR) A green, shiny, wrinkly-skinned vegetable, shaped like a small cucumber. The flavor is cool and slightly bitter due to the quinine content. This is a popular summer vegetable sold fresh and canned. The melon can be seeded, filled with a ground filling and steamed. Use in soups or stir-fry with black beans, pork, chicken or seafood.

BLACK GLUTINOUS RICE Mainly used in sweet dishes, although its color, when cooked, adds contrast to vegetables and protein. The cooking time and water absorption is similar to brown rice. When cooked, the rice has a very fragrant aroma and is deep purple to black in color.

BROCCOLI, CHINESE (GAI LARN) This variety has more leaves and less flowers than European broccoli. It is sold in bunches and can be stir-fried as a vegetable or combined with meats and seafood. Avoid overcooking to preserve the deep fresh green color.

CABBAGE (GAI CHOY) This has a jade green stalk with darker green leaves and is a compact small cabbage with a slight mustard flavor. Cut into 1–2 inch (2–5 cm) pieces and use in clear soups.

CHINESE CABBAGE (BARK CHOY) This cabbage has long white stems and green leaves. Use in stir-fried dishes. The white and green are cut into 1–2 inch (2–5 cm) pieces. The white is stir-fried first in a little oil with ginger, then the green leaf is added with salt and sugar and 3 tbsp (45 mL) stock. Cook covered for a few minutes until bright green and crispy tender.

MUSTARD CABBAGE (CHOY SUM) This is a smaller vegetable than bark choy with similar uses. The stalk and green are cut into 2 inch (5 cm) sections, then blanched and served with oyster sauce. It is a popular restaurant dish. Leaves and stalks are separated for cooking, then cut into sections. The stalk is stir-fried first in a little oil and ginger, then the leaf is added with stock, sugar and salt, and quickly steamed, covered.

CHESTNUT, WATER This root of a marsh plant resembles a small gladiolus bulb. It is often grown as a second crop around the edges of rice fields, as both foods grow in muddy conditions. The chestnut has a crisp, delicate flavor which is similar to apples. The black skin must be peeled off before use and the flesh sliced, diced or minced. Eat raw in salads or include in steamed, deep-fried or stir-fried preparations to give a crisp texture. Water chestnuts are available fresh, and whole or sliced in cans.

CHILI PEPPERS Used fresh or dried to season dishes cooked in the Szechuan style.

CHILI PEPPER SAUCE (CHILI SAUCE) A fiery condiment made with chili peppers, vinegar and seasonings. You may substitute chili paste.

DATES, RED Red dates are used in soups, braised dishes and desserts. They are soaked in warm liquid to plump them before cooking. Sold in packages.

EGG, SALTED DUCK Fresh duck eggs are soaked in a salt brine for 40 days. They must be cooked before eating. Salted eggs can be used for omelets, boiled or steamed on top of rice, braised whole, steamed with pork or used for salty egg cake.

FISH, DRIED SALTED Various sized fish are dried and salted, either whole or in fillets. Slice thinly, place onto a small plate, add 1–3 tbsp (15–45 mL) of vegetable oil and some shredded ginger. Place on top of rice after rice water is absorbed and steam 20 minutes. Eat with rice.

FISH MAW This is the dried and deep-fried stomach lining of fish. Must be

soaked before use. Has no fish flavor when cooked. Used in soup and pork dishes. The large curved crisp pieces are sold by weight.

FIVE-SPICE POWDER A combination of star anise, cloves, fennel, cinnamon and Szechuan pepper used in marinades for roasting pork and poultry. Use sparingly in braised dishes and to flavor breadcrumbs for coating. Sold in small jars and packages.

FRESH GINGER Fresh green ginger root is used extensively in Chinese cooking. It can be pickled, crystallized or preserved in syrup. The dried, ground variety should not be used as a substitute for fresh when cooking Chinese food. Available fresh, or chopped and sliced in jars.

FUNGUS, DRIED BLACK OR WHITE The black variety is called chee yee and, when soaked, can be used in place of mushrooms in soups and stir-fries, or simmered and added to salads. The white variety is cooked in a syrup and served as a dessert called "white cloud".

GINKO NUTS Available in cans for instant use in soups, vegetarian dishes and puddings.

GLUTINOUS FLOUR Ground from glutinous rice, this flour is used for pastries and dough products.

GLUTINOUS RICE (NOR MU) Available white and black. The white comes in whole-grain form and as flour. Use in desserts, pastries, and various dumplings with sweet and savory fillings. When cooked, it is very sticky and is also known as sticky rice throughout Asia.

GOLDEN NEEDLES The dried buds of the tiger lily. When soaked these are used in vegetarian and poultry dishes to add texture and a delicate flavor.

HOISIN SAUCE Also called Peking or barbecue sauce. This thick brownish-red sauce is made from soybeans, spices, garlic and chili peppers. It complements most cooking ingredients – spare ribs, pork, poultry and seafood. It can also be used as a table condiment or a base for dip sauces.

LONGAN (DRAGON EYES) Similar to lychee fruit only smaller. Use in sweet and sour sauces, fruit salad, or appetizer cocktails. Available fresh in season and canned in syrup.

LOTUS LEAVES The leaves from the water lily plant, available fresh and dried. The fresh leaves are used sparingly, sliced in various dishes to impart flavor and fragrance. Dried leaves are soaked before use and are used for wrapping rice, meat and sweet fillings e.g. sweet bean paste, before steaming.

LOTUS ROOT The starchy root of the lotus flower, about 2 inches (5 cm) in diameter. When sliced, reveals an attractive pattern of holes running through the length of the root. Used mainly for soups and in braised dishes. When dried, soaking is required before cooking. Available fresh and canned.

LOTUS SEED PASTE Available in cans, this paste is used as a filling for sweet buns, moon cakes and puddings. The young seed of the water lily can be eaten raw as a fruit or boiled, mashed and sweetened as with the red beans. The seeds are also used in soups, with braised duck, or can be crystallized.

LYCHEE (LICHEE) Grows on a tree in tropical areas. It resembles a round red strawberry with a thin shell-like skin. It has white translucent flesh and one black seed. Sweet and delicate in flavor, it is available fresh and

canned. Used as a dessert with ice cream, in sweet poultry and pork dishes or sweet and sour sauce.

MIXED SPICE Finely ground spice combination, including allspice, nutmeg and cinnamon; used to flavor cakes and buns.

MUSHROOMS, CHINESE Choose the thick black variety. Soak in warm stock or water for 20 minutes to soften. Retain stalk for stock pot. Chinese mushrooms retain their shape in cooking. Can be stir-fried, braised, steamed, chopped and added to rice and poultry stuffings. Store in airtight jar.

MUSHROOMS, STRAW Cultivated on rice straw, these mild-flavored brown, umbrella-shaped mushrooms have a meaty texture. Available canned.

NOODLES, DRIED Dried thin and thick noodles are made from wheat or rice flour, with and without eggs. They are usually cooked in boiling water before frying. Some varieties of rice noodles are soaked in warm water then stir-fried or added to soups. Flavored noodles cook quickly – shrimp, chicken, beef and curry flavors are available.

NOODLES, FRESH Fresh egg and eggless wheat noodles are available in most Chinese supermarkets, in various shapes and sizes. They can be frozen in recipe size amounts. Fresh rice noodles, plain or flavored with shrimp or curry, are available in sheets and strips ready for boiling.

OLIVE NUTS These are the kernels of the Chinese olive and their texture is softer than other nuts used in cooking. They are best toasted to a light ivory color and can be used as a garnish or with mild flavored dishes. They are approximately ½ inch (1 cm) in length.

OYSTER SAUCE Made from fresh oysters, this sauce is used as a flavoring in cooking or served as a table condiment. Available in bottles and cans, it is best to refrigerate after opening.

PARSLEY, CHINESE (CORIANDER) Fresh coriander has a wonderful aroma when crushed or chopped. It can be used fresh, cooked with other ingredients or used as a garnish. Sold fresh in bunches.

PICKLES, CHINESE A combination of ginger, turnip, carrot and cucumber in a pickle brine. Sold in jars.

RED BEANS Small red beans similar in size to mung beans. When cooked, mashed and sweetened the red bean paste is used in sweet buns, desserts, and puddings. The beans are also available in powder form.

RED GINGER Fresh young ginger, peeled, sliced and cooked in a sugar syrup. Available in jars or cans.

RICE Rice is the staple food of southern China. White short-grain is preferred, although brown rice is used in rural areas. Both white and brown rice are available with long and short grains.

RICE PAPERS Thin, transluscent papery sheets made from rice flour.

SAUSAGES, CHINESE, PORK OR LIVER Chinese sausages are sold in pairs or pre-packaged packs. The pork variety is a light pink waxed color; the liver variety is dark. They are both steamed by direct method or on top of rice, before eating or adding to other ingredients.

SESAME OIL Made from sesame seeds, this oil tastes very strong, so use sparingly. Adds flavor to dip sauces, salads, soups, and is rarely used as a cooking oil.

SESAME PASTE, GROUND Toasted sesame seeds, with a peanut butter texture.

Used in sauces and available in cans and jars.

TEMPEH A high-protein food made from soybeans. It has a stronger flavor than tofu, and a firmer, almost meaty texture. Available fresh or frozen.

SOY SAUCE Essential in Chinese cooking to flavor pork, beef, poultry and fish. Available in dark form for cooking and light form for a table condiment. Salt-reduced soy sauce is also available.

SPRING ROLL WRAPPERS Available fresh or frozen in large and small sizes. Fresh wrappers can be re-wrapped and frozen in smaller quantities.

STAR ANISE A dried, star-shaped spice with a licorice-like flavor, used for flavoring meats and poultry.

TANGERINE PEEL, DRIED Tangerine peel which is sun-dried until dark brown and brittle to produce a pungent-flavored seasoning. Sometimes called Mandarin orange peel.

VEGETARIAN MOCK DUCK Made from wheat flour, gluten, safflower oil, soybean extract, sugar, salt and water. Sold in 10 oz (285 g) cans. It is a light food which can replace duck in most recipes.

WONTON WRAPPERS A thin fresh pastry made from eggs and flour. Sold by weight fresh or frozen. Wrappers are 3¼ inches (8 cm) square. Fillings can be make from fresh raw ingredients such as pork, beef, seafood, poultry or vegetables. They can be deep-fried, steamed, boiled or baked. They can be re-wrapped and frozen.

WHEAT STARCH Wheat starch is little used in food preparation but is extensively used as a thickening agent. It has less thickening power and makes a more opaque gel than cornstarch. Its characteristic flavor is preferred by many to that of other thickening agents. It is sold in packages in Chinese food stores.

YUM CHA
AND OTHER APPETIZERS

T his section includes recipes which will tantalize the taste buds
without spoiling your appetite for the main meal to come. Small portions
and light quick cooking are the secret.

Yum cha recipes can form a meal in themselves.
They are a series of little snacks, either steamed or fried, and are
normally eaten at midday as a kind of brunch. This is a meal to be eaten
with a few friends, as the point is to have as big a selection as possible.
The range of choice is enormous.

Dim sum are steamed or fried packages made with wrappers
or skins composed of various kinds of flours, eggs, bean curd, yams,
bread dough or pastry, and wrapped around ground meat or other fillings.

To serve at home, provide a selection of dipping sauces such as
chili, soy, rice vinegar, sesame oil and garlic paste which should be put
in the center of the table.

Tea is the proper drink to have with this snack meal –
the teapot should be refilled as soon as it is empty.

*Fried Pork Patties (page 21), Chicken and Ham Rolls
(page 15) and Lychee Appetizer (page 15)*

PEARL BALLS

1 cup (250 mL) glutinous rice, soaked in cold
water 1 hour

1 lb (450 g) boneless pork with a little fat,
ground

2 tsp (10 mL) ginger wine

3 tbsp (45 mL) light soy sauce

1 egg, beaten

1 tbsp (15 mL) cornstarch

1 green onion, finely chopped

½ tsp (2.5 mL) sugar

¹/₂ tsp (2.5 mL) salt

¼ tsp (1 mL) white pepper

1 Drain rice. Combine pork with remaining ingredients. Shape into 20 balls with
wet hands. Roll each ball in rice until well
coated. Arrange on two heatproof plates.
Leave ½ inch (1 cm) space between each ball
for rice expansion.

2 Steam covered in a steamer basket over
high heat for 1 hour. Serve with prepared
mustard, soy sauce or chili pepper dip.

SERVES 4

❖ **CANNED LYCHEES**

*If using canned lychees,
reserve the lychee juice for
sauces or fruit punch.*

SHRIMP AND PORK DIM SUM

24 wonton wrappers

FILLING

½ lb (225 g) raw shrimp, peeled

½ lb (225 g) lean pork, ground

4 tbsp (60 mL) pork fat, finely chopped

3 Chinese mushrooms, soaked in warm
water 20 minutes

2 oz (60 g) bamboo shoots, diced,
or ½ carrot, shredded

SEASONINGS

3 tbsp (45 mL) oyster sauce

1 tsp (5 mL) salt

2 tsp (10 mL) sugar

2 tsp (10 mL) light soy sauce

½ tsp (2.5 mL) sesame oil

¼ tsp (1 mL) pepper

1 tsp (5 mL) cornstarch

¼ cup (60 mL) water

1 tsp (5 mL) baking soda

1 Wash and devein shrimp and pat dry.
Dice and put into mixing bowl. Add
ground pork and pork fat, mushrooms
without stems and bamboo shoots. Pound
until firm. Add seasonings and pound again
until seasonings are well mixed.

2 Put 2 tsp (10 mL) of filling in each wonton skin. Holding the wrapper in one hand,
squeeze the wrapper around the filling in a
basket shape (see photo, page 17). Using a
knife, flatten the top.

3 Put dim sum in a greased steamer or on a
plate. Steam over high heat for 10 minutes.

MAKES 24

❖ **POUNDING**

*Pounding is done in the bowl with the blunt edge of a
cleaver or a pestle; it gives the mixture a lighter texture
with a slight chew.*

Pearl Balls (page 14) and Bacon-wrapped Water Chestnuts (page 17)

CHICKEN AND HAM ROLLS

2 whole chicken breasts

1 slice ham steak cut ½ inch (1 cm) thick

poultry seasoning

2 tsp (10 mL) hoisin sauce

½ cup (125 mL) all-purpose flour

¼ tsp (1 mL) salt

1 egg, beaten

½ cup (125 mL) milk, or use half water and half milk

1 tbsp (15 mL) cornstarch

1½ cups (375 mL) oil, for deep-frying

1 oz (28 g) vermicelli noodles, deep-fried

1 Remove skin and bone chicken breasts. Place each breast and the small underfillets on a board and cover with foil. Using a rolling pin, press out each chicken piece thinly. Partly cover each breast with the fillet to make an even rectangular shape. Sprinkle with poultry seasoning.

2 Cut ham into four ½ inch (1 cm) wide strips. Spread each strip with hoisin sauce. Place each piece of ham diagonally onto each chicken breast. Roll up and secure with two toothpicks. Chill 15 minutes.

3 Sift flour and salt. Blend in egg and milk to form batter. Sprinkle rolls with cornstarch then coat with batter. Deep-fry two at a time in hot oil until golden. Remove toothpicks and serve sliced and garnished with fried noodles.

SERVES 4

❖ **PREPARATION TIME**

Chinese cooking requires more preparation time than cooking time. Many dishes can actually be cooked in less than 10 minutes. To reduce the preparation time, many convenient ingredients are now available from Oriental food stores and supermarkets. Rice which is available in conventional white or brown, long- or short-grain, can be replaced with the quick-cooking variety in either white or brown, cutting the cooking time in half.

LYCHEE APPETIZER

20 oz (565 g) can lychee fruit, drained

1 tbsp (15 mL) salted cashews, finely chopped

2½ oz (75 g) crabmeat, canned or freshly cooked

1 tbsp (15 mL) mayonnaise

1 tsp (5 mL) light soy sauce

1 green onion, finely cut

2 tsp (10 mL) lemon juice, strained

red ginger or red pepper, for garnish

shredded lettuce

1 Combine cashews, crabmeat, mayonnaise, light soy sauce, green onion and lemon juice. Pack into lychee fruit.

2 Top each with a thin slice of red ginger or red pepper. Arrange on finely shredded lettuce and serve chilled.

SERVES 6–8

STEP-BY-STEP TECHNIQUES

1 *To make spring rolls, you can either use the triangle method (as described in recipe) or use the entire pastry sheet, as shown. Place prepared filling in bottom corner and roll partly closed.*

2 *Fold side corners of wrapper in towards the center.*

3 *Roll up, dampening remaining corner with a little flour and water to seal.*

4 *Deep-fry rolls in a pan or wok, and allow to drain before serving.*

SPRING ROLLS

15 large sheets spring roll pastry

3 Chinese mushrooms, soaked in warm water for 20 minutes, or fresh mushrooms

1 chicken breast fillet, ground

¼ lb (110 g) pork, ground

oil, for frying

½ lb (225 g) water chestnuts, finely chopped

⅓ lb (150 g) bamboo shoots

¼ lb (110 g) Chinese barbecued pork (char sui) or ham, diced

1 small carrot, finely chopped

2½ tbsp (40 mL) all-purpose flour mixed with 2 tbsp (30 mL) water

sweet and sour sauce, to serve

SEASONINGS

3 tbsp (45 mL) oyster sauce

1 tsp (5 mL) salt

2 tsp (10 mL) sugar

2 tsp (10 mL) light soy sauce

1 tsp (5 mL) wine

¼ tsp (1 mL) pepper

¼ tsp (1 mL) sesame oil

1 tbsp (15 mL) cornstarch mixed with 1 tbsp (15 mL) water

❖ **HINT**

Marinate foods overnight for tenderness and flavor.

1 Steam mushrooms, remove stems and finely chop caps. Marinate chicken and pork with 1 tbsp (15 mL) combined seasonings for 10 minutes and set aside. Heat oil in a pan, sauté water chestnuts and bamboo shoots and set aside.

2 Heat another pan with oil and pour in marinated meat and Chinese barbecued pork to sauté. Add mushrooms, carrot, water chestnuts and bamboo shoots, and seasonings. Mix well with combined cornstarch and water and let cool completely before wrapping in pastry.

3 Cut the spring roll sheets diagonally to make triangles. Put each pastry triangle flat on table, place 2 tbsp (30 mL) of filling in center of pastry and fold in two corners to the opposite edge. Roll from the filled end, using flour and water paste to seal the third corner.

4 Pour oil in a heated pan, put spring rolls in hot oil to deep-fry until golden brown. Serve with sweet and sour sauce.

MAKES 30

CHINESE SAUSAGE ROLLS

PASTRY

3 cups (750 mL) all-purpose flour

2 tsp (10 mL) baking powder

½ cup (125 mL) sugar

1 tbsp (15 mL) butter

½–¾ cup (125–185 mL) warm water

½ tsp (2.5 mL) vinegar

FILLING

7 Chinese sausages, washed and halved

1 tbsp (15 mL) oil

1½ tsp (7.5 mL) red bean paste

2 tbsp (30 mL) brown sugar

1 tsp (5 mL) oyster sauce

½ cup (125 mL) water

pinch salt

1 tbsp (15 mL) all-purpose flour

1 Sift flour and baking powder into a bowl. Add sugar and work in butter. Use half the warm water to combine ingredients. Add a little bit more water gradually to work the flour into a dough and knead until smooth. Cover with a damp cloth and set aside for 1½–2 hours until doubled in size.

2 TO MAKE FILLING: Steam Chinese sausages for 7 minutes. Place oil in a pan to heat. Add red bean paste, sugar, oyster sauce, water and salt. Add flour to mixture and stir until lumps disappear. Add sausages and let cool.

3 Roll the soft dough into a sausage-shaped roll. Divide into 14 portions. Press each into rectangular shape, 2 inches (5 cm) wide. Put sausage on one side of pastry and roll towards center. Place on a rectangular piece of wax paper, sealed edge facing down.

4 Place sausage rolls in a steamer and steam over high heat for 12–15 minutes.

MAKES 14

BACON-WRAPPED WATER CHESTNUTS

6 oz (180 g) can whole water chestnuts

3 tbsp (45 mL) hoisin sauce

4–6 slices bacon

1 Drain and dry water chestnuts. Mix with hoisin sauce. Cut each bacon slice into strips long enough to wrap around each chestnut. Secure with toothpick.

2 Arrange on a foil-covered tray. Roast at 425°F (220°C) for 10–15 minutes until bacon is crisp.

SERVES 6

❖ **HINT**

Place cooking ingredients on a tray in order of cooking. This can be done in advance, and the tray kept covered and refrigerated.

❖ **HINT**

Freeze fresh noodles, wonton wrappers and spring roll wrappers in recipe size amounts.

Spring Rolls (page 16), Chinese Sausage Rolls, Shrimp and Pork Dim Sum (page 15)

BEEF AND GREEN ONION FRIED RICE

❖ FRIED RICE

For best results, cook rice the day before, or use leftover rice. Cook as quickly as possible without burning.

1½ tbsp (20 mL) butter

1 lb (450 g) skirt steak, sliced thin

2 cups (500 mL) cold cooked rice

salt and pepper

1 tbsp (15 mL) soy sauce

2 tsp (10 mL) sugar

pinch pepper

3 green onions, finely chopped

1 Melt butter in a wok and stir-fry steak until it has changed color.

2 Add rice and stir-fry over high heat until rice is heated through. Add seasonings and serve decorated with finely chopped green onions.

SERVES 4–6

Silver Pin Noodles with Shredded Chicken and Beef and Green Onion Fried Rice

SILVER PIN NOODLES WITH SHREDDED CHICKEN

1 cup (250 mL) wheat starch

pinch salt

¾ cup (185 mL) boiling water

2 tsp (10 mL) oil

CHICKEN MIXTURE

1 chicken thigh fillet, sliced

½ tsp (2.5 mL) chopped fresh ginger

½ tsp (2.5 mL) Chinese or other white wine

1 tsp (5 mL) cornstarch

oil, for frying

1 Chinese mushroom, soaked in warm water for 20 minutes

1 green onion, chopped

1 clove garlic

1 green pepper, seeded and sliced

1 red pepper, seeded and sliced

¼ lb (110 g) bean sprouts

SEASONINGS

2 tsp (10 mL) oyster sauce

1 tsp (5 mL) sugar

2 tsp (10 mL) soy sauce

¼ tsp (1 mL) sesame oil

1 Sift wheat starch and salt into a mixing bowl. Pour in boiling water and stir. Cover for 5 minutes then remove cover and knead to form a smooth dough.

2 Roll out into a long sausage-shaped roll and cut into 24 equal portions. Knead each portion into the shape of a thin chopstick and cut again into 2 inch (5 cm) portions. Pinch ends to make the noodles pointed. Put silver pin noodles on a greased plate to steam for 5 minutes. When cooked, coat with oil to prevent them from sticking together.

3 Marinate chicken for 20 minutes with ginger, Chinese white wine and cornstarch. Shallow-fry in hot oil 5 minutes and set aside. Steam mushrooms, chop and set aside.

4 Heat pan and add more oil. Sauté briefly green onion, garlic, green and red peppers then bean sprouts. Add chicken meat, silver pin noodles and mushrooms. Sauté together a few minutes, sprinkle with a little more wine, add seasonings and serve hot.

SERVES 4–6

PORK AND LETTUCE ROLLS

Generally, meat filling and lettuce leaves are served separately; guests fill and roll their own lettuce leaves

1 oz (28 g) dried Chinese mushrooms, soaked in warm water 20 minutes

2 tsp (10 mL) oil

¼ lb (110 g) ground pork

2 oz (60 g) water chestnuts, finely chopped

2 oz (60 g) bamboo shoots, finely chopped

3 green onions, finely chopped

7 oz (200 g) can crab, drained and flaked

1 tsp (5 mL) sesame oil

2 tsp (10 mL) soy sauce

1 tsp (5 mL) oyster sauce

1 tbsp (15 mL) sherry

1 head iceberg lettuce, washed and dried

1 Drain mushrooms, remove stems and chop mushroom caps finely.

2 Heat oil in a wok and stir-fry pork until golden. Stir in mushrooms, water chestnuts, bamboo shoots, green onions and crab. Cook 1 minute. Combine sesame oil, soy sauce, oyster sauce and sherry and stir into pork mixture.

3 Place 3 level tbsp (45 mL) of the mixture into the center of each lettuce leaf. Fold in the ends of the lettuce leaf and roll up to form a neat parcel.

SERVES 4

Pork and Lettuce Rolls

❖ NOODLES

Instant noodles are available both plain and flavored with chicken, shrimp, beef, curry or vegetables. They can be used in soups, or stir-fried with other ingredients. Their cooking time of 2 minutes has captured the noodle market. Dried noodles can be boiled then mixed with a small amount of oil and refrigerated in portion sizes up to several days before use.

STEAMED GOW GEES

FILLING

¾ lb (340 g) uncooked shrimp meat or
boneless white fish cut into ¼ inch
(0.5 cm) dice

2 oz (60 g) pork fat, finely chopped

2 oz (60 g) bamboo shoots, finely chopped

½ tsp (2.5 mL) salt

¼ tsp (1 mL) white pepper

½ tsp (2.5 mL) sesame oil

2 tsp (10 mL) cornstarch

DOUGH

1½ cups (375 mL) all-purpose flour or
Chinese gluten-free flour

2 tbsp (30 mL) shortening

1½ cups (375 mL) boiling water

DIP SAUCE I

5 tbsp (75 mL) light soy sauce

2 tsp (10 mL) white vinegar

¼ tsp (1 mL) sesame oil

DIP SAUCE II

3 tbsp (45 mL) tomato catsup

1 tbsp (15 mL) chili pepper sauce

1 Combine filling ingredients. Divide into
36 portions.

2 Sift flour into a bowl. Cut in shortening
and stir in boiling water with a knife to
make dough. Let stand covered until cool.

3 Form dough into a sausage-shaped roll
and cut into 36 even-sized pieces.

4 Roll each piece of dough into a 2 inch
(5 cm) circle on a lightly oiled surface. Place
a portion of filling on each round. Fold
lower edge of dough over filling to form a
half circle. Press edges firmly and pleat
edge.

5 Arrange gow gees on two lightly greased
plates, leaving enough space between each
to prevent sticking. Steam covered for
10–15 minutes. Serve with dip sauce.

6 TO MAKE DIP SAUCE: Combine ingredients for the two sauces in two small bowls.

SERVES 4

❖ **HINT**

*Always make garnishes
before you begin recipe.*

CLOUD SWALLOWS

20 wonton wrappers

1 beaten egg white

oil, for deep-frying

FILLING

¼ lb (110 g) chicken, finely chopped

¼ lb (110 g) fish fillets, finely chopped

½ stalk celery, finely chopped

*Steamed Gow Gees
and Cloud Swallows*

1 small green onion, finely chopped

2 tsp (10 mL) light soy sauce

¼ tsp (1 mL) salt

Sweet and Sour Sauce

¾ cup (185 mL) water

½ cup (125 mL) sugar

½ cup (125 mL) white vinegar

1 tbsp (15 mL) tomato catsup

1 tbsp (15 mL) cornstarch

1 Combine filling ingredients.

2 Place 1 tsp (5 mL) of mixture on each wonton wrapper. Brush edges lightly with egg white. Fold to form a triangle. Place a dab of egg white on the left front corner of triangle. Join the front of the left to the back of the right side of triangle to form a swallow.

3 Deep-fry in oil to cover until golden. Serve with sweet and sour sauce.

4 To Make Sauce: Combine all ingredients in a saucepan. Beat and stir until boiling. Serve in bowls.

Serves 4

FRIED PORK PATTIES

Hot Water Pastry

2½ cups (625 mL) all-purpose flour

¾ cup (185 mL) boiling water

¼ cup (60 mL) cold water (optional)

Filling

1 lb (450 g) pork, finely ground

½ tsp (2.5 mL) salt

pinch white pepper

3 tbsp (45 mL) light soy sauce

½ tsp (2.5 mL) sesame oil

2 green onions, finely chopped

3–4 tbsp (45–60 mL) oil, for frying

Dip Sauce

3 tbsp (45 mL) vegetable oil

1 tbsp (15 mL) light soy sauce

3 tbsp (45 mL) white vinegar

1 tsp (5 mL) sugar

1 Sift flour into a bowl. Stir in boiling water with a knife, adding a little cold water if necessary to take up any excess flour. When cool, knead on lightly floured board until smooth. Cover with a bowl and let rest 30 minutes.

2 Combine pork, salt, pepper, soy sauce, sesame oil and green onions. Chill 30 minutes.

3 Roll out dough with hands to form a sausage-shaped roll. Cut into 20 even portions. Lightly roll each portion into a ball. Roll out each ball into a 4 inch (10 cm) circle, with the edge thinner than the center. The dough circles can be stacked with a piece of wax paper between each. Cover with a bowl to prevent drying out.

4 Divide pork mixture into 20 portions. Place one in center of each piece of dough. Bring the edges together to cover filling. Twist them slightly and pinch to seal.

5 Place seal side down onto board and reshape into a round patty. These may be made in advance and refrigerated.

6 Heat oil in a flat-bottomed pan. Reduce heat and fry patties 4 minutes on each side until brown. Serve hot with dip sauce.

7 To Make Sauce: Warm oil in a saucepan, stir in soy sauce, vinegar and sugar to dissolve. Cool and serve in a small bowl.

Serves 4–6

❖ **Hint**

Toast sesame seeds in a dry pan and store in a jar. Keep a stock of oven-roasted nuts to use as a garnish.

SOUPS

There is an immense variety of soups in Chinese cooking, some light and clear and others thick and filling. They may be bland and served to clear the palate, or spicy and pungent, served as a contrast with other foods.

Most soups have a short cooking time, though some thick and hearty soups, containing dried or salted ingredients for extra flavor, require a longer time.

Green vegetables are usually added in the last few minutes of cooking so they will retain their crispness and bright color. When tougher vegetables like carrots are used, they are parboiled first and then added with the more tender leafy vegetables.

Though some soups are eaten to begin the meal, they are also served as a wonderful accompaniment to rice dishes. There are even a number of sweet soups in Chinese cooking, served only at formal dinners or banquets, which are customarily eaten at the end of a meal.

Wonton Soup (page 26), Chicken Noodle Soup (page 24), and Fish and Spinach Soup (page 24)

CHICKEN NOODLE SOUP

½ lb (225 g) thin long life noodles

1 tbsp (15 mL) light soy sauce

¼ tsp (1 mL) sesame oil

½ lb (225 g) chicken breast, cooked and cut in 2 inch (5 cm) strips

½ bunch fresh mustard cabbage (choy sum), cut in ¾ inch (2 cm) pieces

8 cups (2 L) chicken stock

1 Cook noodles in 4 cups (1 L) boiling salted water for 5 minutes; drain.

2 Place soy sauce and sesame oil in a large soup bowl. Top with cooked noodles. Arrange chicken and cabbage on top. Pour over boiling seasoned stock. Cover and let stand a few minutes before serving.

SERVES 6–8

FISH AND SPINACH SOUP

½ lb (225 g) firm white fish fillets, cut in ¾ x ½ inch (2 x 1 cm) slices

3 tbsp (45 mL) cornstarch seasoned with salt and pepper

6 cups (1.5 L) fish stock

2 tbsp (30 mL) light soy sauce

1 tbsp (15 mL) ginger wine

10 oz (300 g) spinach leaves, cut in ¾ inch (2 cm) pieces

salt and pepper

1 Toss fish slices in cornstarch to coat.

2 Bring stock to a boil. Add soy sauce, wine and fish pieces. Simmer covered for 6 minutes. Add spinach, cook uncovered until bright green, 1–2 minutes. Adjust seasonings and serve.

SERVES 6

BEAN CURD AND VEGETABLE SOUP

6 cups (1.5 L) vegetable stock

1 ripe tomato, skinned, seeded and cut in ½ inch (1 cm) dice

5 button mushrooms, sliced

2 oz (60 g) bean sprouts, root removed

¼ lb (110 g) bean curd, sliced

salt and pepper

1 green onion, finely chopped

1 Bring stock to a boil. Add tomato and mushrooms and simmer for 3 minutes. Add sprouts, bean curd and seasonings. Simmer covered for 2 minutes.

2 Serve with chopped green onions.

SERVES 6

CRAB AND SWEET CORN SOUP

1 tbsp (15 mL) vegetable oil

½ tsp (2.5 mL) chopped fresh ginger

½ lb (225 g) crabmeat, flaked

6 cups (1.5 L) fish stock, seasoned

1 tbsp (15 mL) dry sherry

¾ cup (185 mL) corn kernels

1½ tbsp (20 mL) cornstarch blended with 3 tbsp (45 mL) stock or water

2 egg whites, lightly beaten

chopped green onions, to garnish

1 Heat oil in a wok. Add ginger and crabmeat, stir-fry 2 minutes. Add stock, sherry and corn. When boiling, stir in blended cornstarch and water to thicken. Remove from heat.

2 Pour in egg white in a thin stream. Garnish with green onions.

VARIATION: Children love this soup, especially when chicken is used instead of crab. Simply substitute an equal quantity of chicken stock for fish stock, and chicken for crabmeat.

SERVES 6–8

PEKING HOT SOUR SOUP

4 Chinese mushrooms, soaked in warm water 20 minutes

4 cups (1 L) chicken stock

¼ lb (110 g) lean pork, shredded

2 oz (60 g) canned bamboo shoots, shredded

¼ lb (110 g) bean curd, cut in ½ inch (1 cm) dice

3 tbsp (45 mL) white vinegar

1 tbsp (15 mL) soy sauce

1½ tbsp (20 mL) cornstarch blended with 5 tbsp (75 mL) water

1 egg, beaten

½ tsp (2.5 mL) sesame oil

3 green onions, chopped

1 Squeeze mushrooms dry and remove stems. Cut mushroom caps into thin strips.

2 Bring stock to a boil and add pork and mushrooms. Bring to a boil again, reduce heat and simmer for 8–10 minutes. Add bamboo shoots and bean curd and simmer for another 4–5 minutes.

3 Mix vinegar and soy sauce and stir into soup. Stir in blended cornstarch and water and simmer, stirring constantly, until thickened.

4 Remove from heat and stir in beaten egg. Add sesame oil and green onions and serve hot.

SERVES 4–6

Peking Hot Sour Soup

STEP-BY-STEP TECHNIQUES

1 *To fold wontons: Place ½ tsp (2.5 mL) of filling in wrapper, fold in half and press sides together; fold in half again, pressing firmly at both sides of filling, but leaving corners open.*

2 *Bring two corners together, and cross over in front of filling; where they meet, brush lightly with water or beaten egg, to make them stick.*

WONTON SOUP

WONTONS

2 Chinese mushrooms, soaked in warm water 20 minutes

¼ lb (110 g) lean pork, ground

2 oz (60 g) shrimp meat, minced

2 water chestnuts, very finely chopped

4 green onions, very finely chopped

1 tbsp (15 mL) soy sauce

2 tsp (10 mL) sherry

16 wonton wrappers

1 egg, lightly beaten

SOUP

6 cups (1.5 L) chicken stock

6 green onions, white part only, thinly sliced

1 Squeeze mushrooms dry. Remove stalks and finely chop the caps. Combine mushrooms, pork, shrimp, water chestnuts, green onions, soy sauce and sherry. Let stand 30 minutes.

2 Place ½ tsp (2.5 mL) of filling slightly off center of each wrapper. Fold wrapper in half and press the edges together to seal them. Again, fold the wrapper in half. Pull the corners down into a crescent shape, overlapping the corners. Seal the overlap with a little beaten egg.

3 Drop the wontons one by one into boiling salted water and simmer 7 minutes, making sure they do not stick to the bottom of the pan. Drain the wontons. Bring chicken stock to a boil and add wontons and green onions.

SERVES 6–8

Wonton Soup

PORK AND SHRIMP SOUP

¾ lb (340 g) egg noodles, cooked

4 tbsp (60 mL) oil

1 small onion, peeled and thinly sliced

2 slices fresh ginger, finely chopped

½ lb (225 g) lean pork, finely shredded

2 oz (60 g) Chinese mushrooms, soaked in warm water 20 minutes and shredded

½ Chinese cabbage, shredded and blanched

¼ lb (110 g) bean sprouts

¼ lb (110 g) shrimp

3 tbsp (45 mL) soy sauce

4 cups (1 L) beef or chicken stock

1 Heat oil in a wok. Add onion, ginger and pork and stir-fry for 2 minutes.

2 Add mushrooms, cabbage, bean sprouts and shrimp; stir-fry for 2 minutes. Stir in soy sauce and stir-fry a further 1½ minutes. Remove from heat and keep warm.

3 Bring stock to a boil. Add half the pork mixture and bring to a boil again. Add noodles and heat through. Serve soup topped with remaining hot pork mixture.

SERVES 6

Pork and Shrimp Soup

❖ HINT

Place cooking ingredients on a tray in order of cooking. This can be done in advance, and kept covered and refrigerated.

SEAFOOD

The aim in cooking fish is to produce as natural a
flavor as possible from the freshest fish available.
Steaming as well as clear simmering are favorite ways of cooking
fish because the subtle natural flavor is retained and
the flesh is both tender and moist. However, deep-frying,
braising and even stir-frying are methods which are also used.

Fish which is to be deep-fried is either dredged in
flour or cornstarch or is coated with a batter to seal in all of the juices.
To eliminate the 'fishy' taste, a number of seasonings
can be used with the fish. Ginger, garlic, green onions,
black beans, soy sauce and wine are the most popular.
The fish is often scored to permit the flavors to be absorbed
better and to expose a greater cooking surface.

Besides fish, the Chinese also eat a great deal of other seafood
including shrimp, crab, lobster, scallops, clams and oysters.
They are also fond of sea cucumber, squid and sea urchins.

Though fresh seafood is generally preferable,
frozen seafood can be substituted successfully. Canned abalone
need only be heated very briefly.

Sizzling Mongolian Scallops and
Combination Seafood in Nests (page 30)

COMBINATION SEAFOOD IN NESTS

❖ SQUID

To prepare squid, remove the outer purple membrane. Place knife into tube and cut through at one edge. Open out tube. Score the inner surface in a small diamond pattern. This acts as a tenderizer and enables the squid strips to curl when being stir-fried. Cut squid into 1½ x ¾ inch (4 x 2 cm) strips for cooking.

4 tbsp (60 mL) vegetable oil

½ tsp (2.5 mL) salt

½ tsp (2.5 mL) chopped fresh ginger

¼ lb (110 g) scallops

¼ lb (110 g) prepared squid cut into rings

¼ lb (110 g) uncooked shrimp, peeled and deveined

¼ lb (110 g) firm white fish, cut in 1 inch (2.5 cm) dice

½ tsp (2.5 mL) chopped garlic

¼ lb (110 g) broccoli florets

¼ lb (110 g) snow peas, stems removed

2 oz (60 g) Chinese cabbage, stems cut in 1¼ x ½ inch (3 x 1 cm) pieces

1 oz (28 g) bamboo shoots, sliced

1 oz (28 g) canned mini corn

½ oz (14 g) button mushrooms, sliced

½ oz (14 g) straw mushrooms

1 tbsp (15 mL) light soy sauce

3 tbsp (45 mL) dry sherry

1 tsp (5 mL) sugar

pinch pepper

½ cup (125 mL) fish stock

3 tbsp (45 mL) oyster sauce

1 tbsp (15 mL) cornstarch

¼ cup (60 mL) water or stock

1 Heat half the oil. Add salt and ginger, and stir-fry 30 seconds. Add seafood and cook 2 minutes. Remove from pan.

2 Heat remaining oil, add garlic, broccoli, snow peas and cabbage stems. Stir-fry 2 minutes. Add chopped cabbage leaves, bamboo shoots, corn, mushrooms and straw mushrooms. Blend in soy sauce, sherry, sugar, pepper and stock.

3 Combine oyster sauce, cornstarch and water. Bring vegetables and sauce to a boil, and stir in cornstarch mixture to thicken. Fold in seafood to reheat.

4 Serve in noodle nests.

SERVES 4

SIZZLING MONGOLIAN SCALLOPS

For this recipe you will need a sizzle plate, which consists of an iron plate that fits into a thick wooden mold of similar shape. Heat the iron plate on top of your stove for 5 minutes before adding cooked ingredients.

1 lb (450 g) scallops

1 tbsp (15 mL) light soy sauce

1 tbsp (15 mL) dry sherry

3 tbsp (45 mL) vegetable oil

1 large onion, peeled and cut in eighths

1 tsp (5 mL) chopped fresh ginger

SAUCE

1 tsp (5 mL) chili garlic sauce

2 tsp (10 mL) hoisin sauce

1 tsp (5 mL) sesame oil

½ tsp (2.5 mL) five-spice powder

1 tsp (5 mL) sugar

1 tbsp (15 mL) peanut butter

¼ cup (60 mL) fish stock

1 In a bowl combine scallops, soy sauce and sherry. Heat oil in a wok. Add onion and stir-fry 1 minute. Add ginger, scallops and marinade, stir-fry 2−3 minutes.

2 Blend in sauce ingredients and stir-fry until boiling. Serve at once on hot sizzle plate.

SERVES 6

❖ NOODLES

Instant noodles are available both plain and flavored with chicken, shrimp, beef, curry or vegetables. They can be used in soups, or stir-fried with a topping. Their cooking time of 2 minutes has captured the noodle market. Dried noodles can be boiled then mixed with a small amount of oil and refrigerated in portion sizes several days before use.

STEP-BY-STEP TECHNIQUES

STIR-FRIED SQUID AND VEGETABLES

1½ lbs (700 g) squid

3 Chinese mushrooms soaked in warm water 20 minutes

1 bunch Chinese spinach or cabbage

4 tbsp (60 mL) oil

1 onion

¼ tsp (1 mL) grated fresh ginger

2 oz (60 g) bamboo shoots

¼ lb (110 g) carrots, finely sliced

¼ lb (110 g) green beans, finely chopped

¼ lb (110 g) red or green pepper, finely sliced

½ cup (125 mL) chicken stock

1 tbsp (15 mL) soy sauce

2 tsp (10 mL) cornstarch blended with 1½ tbsp (20 mL) water

1 Pull tentacles and intestines out of squid. Pull 'feather' out of body and discard. Cut tentacles from intestines, discard intestines. Rinse body and tentacles and peel skin from body. Drain well. Halve bodies lengthwise and score the inner surface.

2 Discard mushroom stalks and slice caps.

3 Cut spinach into 2 inch (5 cm) strips. Parboil stalks for 3 minutes, drain and refresh under cold running water. Halve onion lengthwise then cut into 4 lengthwise strips. Separate into layers. Slice bamboo shoots.

4 Heat oil in a wok. Stir-fry squid 1 minute. Add onion and stir-fry for 30 seconds.

5 Add ginger, spinach, mushrooms, bamboo shoots, carrot, beans and red or green pepper and stir-fry a further 30 seconds. Pour in chicken stock and soy sauce. Bring to a boil, reduce heat and simmer, covered, 3 minutes.

6 Stir combined cornstarch and water into sauce and cook until thickened.

SERVES 4

1 Pull tentacles and intestines out of squid. Pull 'feather' out of squid and discard, as shown.

2 Rinse body and tentacles and peel skin from body. Drain well. Halve body lengthwise and score surface.

Shrimp Chow Mein

CRABMEAT SAUCE OVER BROCCOLI

1 tbsp (15 mL) vegetable oil

1 slice fresh ginger

1 clove garlic, crushed

1⅔ lbs (750 g) broccoli florets

¼ tsp (1 mL) salt

1 tsp (5 mL) light soy sauce

½ tsp (2.5 mL) sugar

3 tbsp (45 mL) dry sherry

¼ cup (60 mL) fish stock or water

SAUCE

1 tbsp (15 mL) dry sherry or white wine

¼ tsp (1 mL) salt

pinch pepper

1 cup (250 mL) fish stock

1½ tbsp (20 mL) cornstarch blended with
3 tbsp (45 mL) stock or water

½ lb (225 g) crabmeat, fresh, frozen
or canned

1 tbsp (15 mL) shredded red pepper,
blanched

1 Heat oil in a wok. Add ginger and garlic and cook until golden; remove. Add broccoli, stirring to coat with oil. Stir in salt, soy sauce, sugar, sherry and stock. Cook covered for 3–4 minutes until broccoli is bright green. Avoid overcooking.

2 Remove to serving platter and keep warm.

3 TO MAKE SAUCE: Heat sherry, salt, pepper and stock. Stir in blended cornstarch and stock to thicken. When boiling, stir in crabmeat. Simmer 2–3 minutes. Pour sauce over broccoli, garnish with red pepper and serve.

SERVES 4–6

SHRIMP CHOW MEIN

10 Chinese mushrooms, soaked in warm
water 20 minutes

3 tbsp (45 mL) oil

2 stalks celery, sliced

4 oz (110 g) bamboo shoots, sliced

½ lb (225 g) bean sprouts, washed

½ lb (225 g) water chestnuts, drained
and sliced

½ cup (125 mL) chicken stock

1 tbsp (15 mL) dry sherry

1 tbsp (15 mL) soy sauce

1 lb (450 g) shrimp, peeled

❖ **HINT**

*Blend a large quantity
of cornstarch with water
in a jar. Store in
refrigerator and shake
jar to mix before using.*

1 Drain mushrooms, squeeze dry and discard stalks. Slice caps into strips. Heat oil in a wok. Add celery, bamboo shoots, mushrooms, bean sprouts and water chestnuts. Stir-fry about 2 minutes until vegetables are tender but crisp.

2 Pour in stock and sherry. Increase heat to high and bring to a boil. Reduce heat and stir in soy sauce and shrimp. Cover and cook for 3 minutes. Remove from heat and serve immediately.

SERVES 4

BUTTERFLY SHRIMP

5 tbsp (75 mL) all-purpose flour

½ tsp (2.5 mL) salt

1 egg, beaten

5 tbsp (75 mL) beer or water

12 uncooked jumbo shrimp

12 bacon pieces ½ x 2 inches (1 x 5 cm)

24 small broccoli florets, blanched

**3 tbsp (45 mL) cornstarch seasoned
with salt and pepper**

**1½ cups (375 mL) vegetable oil,
for deep-frying**

lemon wedges, to serve

1 Sift flour and salt. Stir in egg and beer to form batter.

2 Shell and devein shrimp, retaining tail.

Cut shrimp through center lengthwise to the tail, but not through the tail. Wrap one strip of bacon around tail end of each shrimp. Fasten with toothpick. Place one broccoli floret on each end of toothpick. Bend each shrimp half around broccoli and fasten onto toothpick. Sprinkle shrimp with cornstarch. Lightly coat with batter. Do not batter the tail.

3 Heat oil. Fry shrimp one at a time until tail turns pink, 2–3 minutes. Drain well. Serve with lemon and dip sauce of your choice.

SERVES 2

Butterfly Shrimp

WHOLE FISH IN BLACK BEAN SAUCE

1⅔ lb (750 g) whole fish, cleaned and scaled (fish cutlets or fillets can also be used)

½ tsp (2.5 mL) salt

1 tbsp (15 mL) all-purpose flour

½ cup (125 mL) vegetable oil

½ tsp (2.5 mL) chopped fresh ginger

½ tsp (2.5 mL) chopped garlic

1 tbsp (15 mL) fermented black beans, chopped

2 tsp (10 mL) dry sherry

2 tsp (10 mL) soy sauce

½ tsp (2.5 mL) sugar

1 cup (250 mL) fish stock or water

2 tsp (10 mL) cornstarch blended with 1½ tbsp (20 mL) water

2 medium green onions, chopped

1 tbsp (15 mL) shredded red pepper, blanched 1 minute in boiling water

1 Score fish on both sides. Season lightly with salt, then coat with flour.

2 Heat oil in a pan. Add fish and fry on both sides until golden. Remove to serving plate and keep hot. Pour off excess oil from pan leaving 1 tbsp (15 mL). Reheat, add ginger, garlic and beans, stir-fry 1 minute. Stir in sherry, soy sauce, sugar and stock. When boiling stir in blended cornstarch and water to thicken.

3 Add green onions. Spoon over fish and garnish with red pepper.

SERVES 6

STIR-FRIED CRAB, GINGER AND GREEN ONIONS

2 large live crabs

3 tbsp (45 mL) oil

1 clove garlic, crushed

3 thin slices fresh ginger, finely chopped

1 bunch green onions, sliced

¾ cup (185 mL) chicken stock

1 tbsp (15 mL) soy sauce

1 tbsp (15 mL) sherry

¼ tsp (1 mL) sugar

dash sesame oil

2 tsp (10 mL) cornstarch blended with 3 tbsp (45 mL) water

1 Cut crabs in half and segment them. Heat oil in a wok. Add garlic, ginger and green onions, and stir-fry for 30 seconds. Add crab pieces and stir-fry to coat with oil. Pour in stock, soy sauce, sherry, sugar and sesame oil and bring to a boil.

2 Cook covered until crab shells turn pink. Stir in blended cornstarch, bring to a boil and serve.

SERVES 4

❖ **HINT**

Chinese cooking requires more preparation time than cooking time. Many dishes can actually be cooked in less than 10 minutes. To reduce the preparation time, many convenient ingredients are now available from Oriental food stores and supermarkets. Rice, which is available in conventional white or brown, long- or short-grain, can be replaced with the quick-cooking variety in either white or brown, cutting the cooking time in half.

SIMMERED WHOLE FISH

2 lbs (1 kg) whole fish

6 cups (1.5 L) water

2 green onions, cut in large pieces

2 thin slices fresh ginger, finely chopped

3 tbsp (45 mL) sherry

1 tbsp (15 mL) soy sauce

5 tbsp (75 mL) oil

4 green onions, sliced thinly

2 slices red ginger, thinly sliced

3 tbsp (45 mL) soy sauce

1 tsp (5 mL) sesame oil

1 Scale fish, leaving head and tail intact. Score, rinse under cold water and drain.

2 Bring water to a boil. Add green onions, ginger, sherry, soy sauce and 3 tbsp (45 mL) oil to the water, and return to boil.

3 Place fish on a wire-mesh strainer and lower into the boiling liquid. Reduce heat, cover and simmer gently 5 minutes. Turn off heat completely and leave, covered, for 20–25 minutes. Remove the fish carefully onto a serving platter. Sprinkle with finely sliced green onions, red ginger and soy sauce. Heat remaining 2 tbsp (30 mL) oil with sesame oil until sizzling, and pour over fish.

SERVES 4

Whole Fish in Black Bean Sauce

CRAB FOO YUNG

4 eggs

1 tsp (5 mL) soy sauce

½ tsp (2.5 mL) chili pepper sauce

2 tsp (10 mL) sherry

½ lb (225 g) fresh or canned crabmeat

4 tbsp (60 mL) oil

6 Chinese mushrooms, soaked in warm water 20 minutes

6 green onions, finely diced

SAUCE

1 cup (250 mL) chicken stock

2 tsp (10 mL) soy sauce

1½ tbsp (20 mL) cornstarch blended with 1½ tbsp (20 mL) water

1 Beat eggs lightly in a bowl. Stir in soy and chili pepper sauces with sherry. Shred crabmeat.

2 Heat 1 tbsp (15 mL) oil in a wok. Discard mushroom stalks and slice caps. Stir-fry mushrooms and green onions for 2 minutes; add crabmeat and stir-fry 1 minute.

3 Remove wok from heat. Remove the mixture to a bowl, cool a few minutes and combine with egg mixture.

4 Heat 3 tbsp (45 mL) oil in wok. Add a quarter of mixture and cook until the omelet is just set and lightly browned on the underside. Turn and cook for 1 minute. Place omelet on a serving plate. Repeat to make a total of 4 omelets.

5 TO MAKE SAUCE: Bring stock, soy sauce and blended cornstarch and water to a boil, stirring constantly. Simmer 1 minute.

SERVES 2

FISH BALLS

2 lbs (1 kg) firm white, unfrozen fish fillets

2 eggs

1 tbsp (15 mL) ginger wine

2 tsp (10 mL) cornstarch

½ tsp (2.5 mL) salt

pinch white pepper

stock or water

Crab Foo Yung

1 Cut fish into ¾ inch (2 cm) cubes. Blend in a food processor with remaining ingredients except stock or water. Shape mixture into ¾ inch (2 cm) balls, with wet hands. Add balls to boiling stock or water to cover. Cook over medium heat 4 minutes, drain. Once cooked, fish balls will keep refrigerated for several days. Use in soups, add to stir-fried seafood combinations or deep-fry and serve with various sauces.

MAKES APPROXIMATELY 20

BRAISED ABALONE WITH CHINESE CABBAGE

1 tbsp (15 mL) vegetable oil

1 tsp (5 mL) chopped fresh ginger

½ tsp (2.5 mL) chopped garlic

1 lb (450 g) mustard cabbage (choy sum), cut into 2 inch (5 cm) lengths

1 tsp (5 mL) sugar

2 tsp (10 mL) dry sherry

½ cup (125 mL) reserved canned abalone liquid

1 tsp (5 mL) sesame oil

1 tbsp (15 mL) oyster sauce

1 tbsp (15 mL) soy sauce

2 tsp (10 mL) cornstarch

¼ cup (60 mL) water

20 oz (560 g) can abalone, drained and thinly sliced (retain liquid)

1 Heat oil. Add ginger, garlic and cabbage stems. Stir-fry 1 minute. Add cabbage leaves, sugar, sherry and abalone liquid. Cook until cabbage is bright green. Arrange cabbage on serving platter and keep warm.

2 Add sesame oil, oyster and soy sauces to pan. Combine cornstarch with water. Stir into boiling sauce. Reduce heat and fold in abalone slices to heat through briefly. Extended cooking will toughen abalone. Arrange slices over cabbage. Spoon sauce on top and serve at once.

SERVES 6–8

HONEYED SHRIMP

3 tbsp (45 mL) oil

1 clove garlic, crushed

1 slice fresh ginger, finely chopped

1⅔ lbs (750 g) uncooked shrimp, peeled with tail intact

¼ cup (60 mL) honey

2 tsp (10 mL) soy sauce

sesame seeds

1 Heat oil in a wok. Add garlic and ginger and stir-fry for 30 seconds. Add shrimp in two batches and stir-fry until pink. Remove the first batch before cooking the second. Pour over combined honey and soy sauce, toss quickly.

2 Serve sprinkled with sesame seeds.

SERVES 4

Braised Abalone with Chinese Cabbage

MEAT

Chinese cooking uses rice and noodles as the basic
staples of each meal, fleshed out with vegetables and garnished
with meat. Western tastes have traditionally been more accustomed
to larger quantities of meat, but Chinese recipes are now appreciated for
providing an inexpensive, nutritious and healthy balance of
ingredients with an amazing variety of flavors provided
by exotic but easily obtainable spices and herbs.
Beef, lamb and pork are the main kinds of meat used and often
form the centerpiece of a special celebratory occasion. The techniques
include steaming, simmering, braising, toasting and stir-frying.

Spicy Beef Satay and Cantonese Beef (page 40)

SLICED BEEF WITH OYSTER SAUCE

2 tbsp (30 mL) vegetable oil

½ tsp (2.5 mL) chopped garlic

1 lb (450 g) boneless steak, thinly sliced

1 tsp (5 mL) soy sauce

1 tbsp (15 mL) dry sherry

¾ cup (185 mL) beef stock

1 tbsp (15 mL) cornstarch

3 tbsp (45 mL) oyster sauce

1 tsp (5 mL) soy sauce

1 tsp (5 mL) sugar

½ tsp (2.5 mL) salt

1 Heat oil in a pan. Add garlic and stir briefly. Add a third of beef. Stir-fry 1 minute until it changes color. Remove and repeat with remaining slices.

2 Return beef to pan. Add soy sauce and sherry, and cook for 1 minute. Pour in ½ cup (125 mL) stock.

3 Blend cornstarch with oyster sauce, remaining stock, soy sauce, sugar and salt. Stir in to thicken. Serve at once.

SERVES 6

SPICY BEEF SATAY

1 lb (450 g) boneless steak, cut in thin strips

1 tbsp (15 mL) soy sauce

1 tsp (5 mL) sesame oil

2 tsp (10 mL) curry paste

4 tbsp (60 mL) sesame paste

3 tbsp (45 mL) dry sherry

3 tbsp (45 mL) vegetable oil

1 Combine steak with soy sauce and sesame oil. Marinate 15 minutes.

2 Thread three to four slices on each satay stick. Leave ¾ inch (2 cm) at the pointed end of stick without meat. A thin strip of foil can be wound around the blunt end of each stick to decorate.

3 Combine curry paste, sesame paste and sherry. Spread thinly over beef. Brush with oil and cook under a preheated broiler 1–2 minutes on each side.

SERVES 4

CANTONESE BEEF

5 tbsp (75 mL) vegetable oil

2 medium onions, peeled and finely shredded

4 large tomatoes, peeled, cut in eighths

1 tsp (5 mL) sugar

½ tsp (2.5 mL) salt

1 tbsp (15 mL) fermented black beans, chopped

1 tsp (5 mL) chopped fresh ginger

1 tsp (5 mL) chopped garlic

1 lb (450 g) boneless steak, cut in thin strips

3 tbsp (45 mL) soy sauce

1 cup (250 mL) beef stock

1½ tbsp (20 mL) cornstarch blended with 2½ tbsp (40 mL) stock or water

green tops of green onions, sliced

1 Heat 3 tbsp (45 mL) oil. Add onions, stir-fry 2 minutes. Add tomatoes, sugar and salt; stir-fry 1 minute. Cover and cook until tomatoes are just tender and retain shape. Remove to a bowl.

2 Heat remaining oil, add black beans, ginger and garlic. Stir-fry 1 minute. Add beef and cook over high heat until color changes, 2–3 minutes. Add soy sauce, tomato mixture and beef stock.

3 Stir in blended cornstarch and stock to thicken, without breaking tomato pieces. Serve garnished with green onion tops.

SERVES 6

❖ **HINT**

To slice steak, cut into three or four portions. Place in freezer until firm. Cut thinly into diagonal slices.

❖ **HINT**

Soak bamboo satay sticks in water so they won't burn.

STEP-BY-STEP TECHNIQUES

STEAMED BEEF BALLS WITH WATER CHESTNUTS

1 cup (250 mL) uncooked rice

1 lb (450 g) round steak, minced

3 green onions, finely chopped

1 tsp (5 mL) finely chopped fresh ginger

2 water chestnuts, finely chopped

1 egg, lightly beaten

1 tbsp (15 mL) soy sauce

3 tbsp (45 mL) sherry

green vegetable leaves

soy sauce and chili pepper sauce, to serve

1 Place rice in a bowl, cover with water and soak for 1–1½ hours. Drain well and spread out on a tray to dry.

2 Combine steak, green onions, ginger, water chestnuts, egg, soy sauce and sherry; mix until well blended. Form mixture into balls about 1½ inches (4 cm) in diameter.

3 Roll each ball in rice until completely covered. Place balls on green vegetables in a steamer basket, leaving enough space between so they don't touch each other.

4 Place in a steamer and steam for 30 minutes over gently boiling water. Serve with soy and chili pepper sauces for dipping.

SERVES 4

1 *Prepare fresh ingredients by chopping finely. Form mixture into balls and roll in rice to coat.*

2 *Place balls on green leafy vegetables in a steamer basket, leaving space between balls so they don't touch.*

Steamed Beef Balls with Water Chestnuts

*For best results, buy
round steak and mince it
yourself. There are two
methods of grinding.*

*Trim the meat and cut
into largish pieces. Use
one or two cleavers, one in
each hand, and keep
chopping until the meat is
minced. Place a damp
kitchen cloth under the
board to dampen the noise.*

*Trim the meat and grind
in a food processor or use a
meat grinder.*

BEEF WITH SNOW PEAS

1 lb (450 g) snow peas

4 tbsp (60 mL) oil

2 tsp (10 mL) oyster sauce

1 lb (450 g) rump steak

2 cloves garlic, peeled and finely chopped

2 thin slices fresh ginger, shredded

1 tbsp (15 mL) soy sauce

1 red chili pepper, seeded and sliced

1 Top and tail snow peas and wipe with a damp cloth if necessary. Heat 1 tbsp (15 mL) oil in a wok, add snow peas and stir-fry 1 minute. Add oyster sauce and toss to coat. Remove and keep warm.

2 Trim meat and cut into four pieces. Heat remaining oil, add meat, garlic and ginger and cook until meat is sealed on both sides. Remove and cut meat into strips. Return to the wok and continue stir-frying for a further 5 minutes. Sprinkle with soy sauce. Serve topped with sliced chili pepper.

NOTE: If snow peas are not in season, Chinese broccoli or spinach may be substituted.

SERVES 4

GINGERED BEEF

1 tsp (5 mL) grated fresh ginger

⅓ cup (85 mL) soy sauce

2 tsp (10 mL) cornstarch

1 lb (450 g) rump steak, trimmed and thinly sliced across the grain

4 Chinese mushrooms, soaked in warm water 20 minutes

¼ cup (60 mL) oil

2 inch (5 cm) piece fresh ginger, shredded

4 oz (110 g) canned bamboo shoots, drained and diced

1 In a large bowl combine grated ginger, soy sauce and cornstarch.

2 Add meat and mix well. Allow to marinate for 1 hour, stirring occasionally. Drain mushrooms, remove stems and discard. Slice mushroom caps.

3 Remove meat from marinade and reserve. Heat oil in a wok over moderate heat. Add ginger and stir-fry for 3 minutes. Add meat, bamboo shoots and mushrooms and stir-fry until meat is cooked. Add marinade and heat through. Serve with rice or boiled noodles.

SERVES 4

CELLOPHANE BEEF

*Each diner breaks open the envelopes with chopsticks
and eats the contents from the wrapper.*

⅓ lb (150 g) beef fillet

7 x 6 inch (18 x 15 cm) squares rice paper

1 tbsp (15 mL) sesame oil

18 thin rings of carrot, parboiled

6 snow peas, stems removed, cut into thirds

1 medium onion, peeled and finely chopped

oil, for deep-frying

shredded lettuce, to serve

MARINADE

½ tsp (2.5 mL) chopped garlic

¼ cup (60 mL) soy sauce

1 tbsp (15 mL) dry sherry

½ tsp (2.5 mL) sugar

¼ tsp (1 mL) pepper

1 tbsp (15 mL) vegetable oil

1 Chill beef and cut into 18 thin slices.

2 Combine garlic, soy sauce, sherry, sugar, pepper and oil. Add beef and stir to coat. Marinate 1 hour. Discard marinade.

3 Lay out rice paper sheets with one corner pointing towards you. Brush each sheet lightly with sesame oil. Place one slice of carrot, snow pea and ½ tsp (2.5 mL) onion in center of lower half of paper. Top with one slice of beef. Fold up lower corner to

cover beef. Fold left and right corners to center. Fold lower section up once more to center line. Fold top corner down like an envelope and tuck in securely. Repeat until all the packages are made.

4 Heat oil to 300°F (150°C). Deep-fry a few envelopes at a time for 5 minutes. Drain well and arrange three envelopes each on six plates of shredded lettuce.

SERVES 6

FILLET STEAK CHINESE-STYLE

¾ lb (340 g) piece beef fillet

1 tbsp (15 mL) soy sauce

1 tbsp (15 mL) hoisin sauce

1 tbsp (15 mL) dry sherry

pinch five-spice powder

3 tbsp (45 mL) vegetable oil

¼ tsp (1 mL) salt

1 large onion, peeled and cut into eighths

½ tsp (2.5 mL) chopped fresh ginger

1 tsp (5 mL) chopped garlic

1 level tbsp (15 mL) cornstarch

¼ cup (60 mL) beef stock

½ tsp (2.5 mL) sesame oil

green onion tops, to serve

1 Freeze beef briefly until firm, then cut into thin slices.

2 Combine beef, soy and hoisin sauces, sherry and five-spice, and marinate for 15 minutes. Remove beef and set marinade aside.

3 Heat 1 tbsp (15 mL) oil in a pan. Add salt and onion and stir-fry 1 minute. Remove onion with a slotted spoon and set aside. Heat remaining oil in pan and add ginger, garlic and beef. Stir-fry 1–2 minutes, until beef just loses its pinkness. Do not overcook or it will become tough. Return onion to pan.

4 Blend cornstarch and stock and stir in to thicken. Sprinkle sesame oil on top and serve garnished with sliced tops of green onions.

SERVES 6

Fillet Steak Chinese-style

DEEP-FRIED SZECHUAN PORK

**2 lbs (1 kg) pork ribs, cut in
1 inch (2.5 cm) squares**

2 tsp (10 mL) chopped fresh ginger

5 tbsp (75 mL) brown sugar

¼ cup (60 mL) soy sauce

3 tbsp (45 mL) dry sherry

½ tsp (2.5 mL) five-spice powder

1½ cups (375 mL) vegetable oil

SZECHUAN SAUCE

3 tbsp (45 mL) vegetable oil

3 red chili peppers, chopped

2 tsp (10 mL) chopped ginger

2 tsp (10 mL) chopped garlic

½ medium onion, peeled and chopped

3 tbsp (45 mL) dry sherry

5 tbsp (75 mL) sugar

5 tbsp (75 mL) tomato catsup

5 tbsp (75 mL) white vinegar

1 Place ribs in a saucepan, cover with cold water and bring to a boil. Simmer 30 minutes; drain well.

2 Combine ginger, sugar, soy sauce, sherry and five-spice powder. Add ribs, stirring to coat. Marinate 3 hours; drain and discard marinade.

3 Heat oil. Deep-fry ribs in small amounts until golden and tender. Drain well.

4 TO MAKE SAUCE: Heat oil in a pan. Add chili peppers, ginger, garlic and onion. Fry until tender. Add sherry, sugar, catsup and vinegar. Simmer 10–15 minutes.

5 Add ribs, stirring to coat well. Simmer 10 minutes and serve hot.

SERVES 6

PORK BALLS WITH GINGER

**8 dried Chinese mushrooms, soaked
in warm water 20 minutes**

1⅔ lbs (750 g) lean pork, ground

**1 inch (2.5 cm) piece fresh ginger,
finely chopped**

4 canned water chestnuts, finely chopped

1 egg

1 tbsp (15 mL) soy sauce

5 tbsp (75 mL) cornstarch

½ cup (125 mL) oil

1 bamboo shoot, diced

1 red pepper, diced

1 green pepper, diced

SAUCE

½ cup (125 mL) vinegar

½ cup (125 mL) sherry

3 tbsp (45 mL) sugar

3 tbsp (45 mL) tomato catsup

¼–½ tsp (1–2.5 mL) chili pepper sauce

1 tbsp (15 mL) soy sauce

**1 tbsp (15 mL) cornstarch blended with
3 tbsp (45 mL) water**

1 Drain mushrooms, discard stems and slice caps finely.

2 Combine ground pork with ginger, water chestnuts, egg, soy sauce and half the cornstarch. Shape into small balls and roll in remaining cornstarch.

3 Heat ⅓ cup (85 mL) oil in a wok. Fry pork balls in batches until crisp and brown. Test one to see if it is cooked. Remove and drain on paper towels.

4 Combine all sauce ingredients except cornstarch paste.

5 Heat 3 tbsp (45 mL) oil in the wok and stir-fry all the vegetables for 3 minutes. Pour in sauce and cook for a further 3 minutes. Thicken with cornstarch paste. Pour vegetables and sauce over pork balls.

SERVES 4

*Pork Balls with
Ginger and Deep-fried
Szechuan Pork*

*Braised Pork Fillet
in Peking Sauce*

BRAISED PORK
FILLET IN PEKING
SAUCE

1 lb (450 g) pork fillets, thinly sliced

1 tsp (5 mL) cornstarch

1 tbsp (15 mL) soy sauce

1 tbsp (15 mL) dry sherry

1 tbsp (15 mL) stock

**¾ lb (340 g) Chinese spinach, blanched
in boiling stock for 1 minute**

3 tbsp (45 mL) vegetable oil

3 tbsp (45 mL) hoisin sauce

½ tsp (2.5 mL) sesame oil or seeds

1 Combine pork with cornstarch,
soy sauce, sherry and stock. Let stand
15 minutes. Chop spinach, arrange on a
serving platter and keep warm.

2 Heat oil in a wok. Stir-fry pork for 2–3
minutes. Remove from oil.

3 Reheat oil, add hoisin sauce. When hot,
return pork. Stir-fry to reheat and coat with
sauce. Add sesame oil. Serve over spinach.

SERVES 4–6

SWEET AND
SOUR PORK

**1 lb (450 g) lean pork, cut in
¾ inch (2 cm) cubes**

½ tsp (2.5 mL) salt

1 tbsp (15 mL) all-purpose flour

1 tsp (5 mL) dry sherry

1 egg yolk

½ cup (125 mL) cornstarch

1 tbsp (15 mL) vegetable oil

1 tsp (5 mL) chopped fresh ginger

1 tsp (5 mL) chopped garlic

½ red pepper, cut in ¾ inch (2 cm) dice

½ green pepper, cut in ¾ inch (2 cm) dice

⅓ lb (150 g) Chinese mixed pickles, sliced

½ cup (125 mL) water

1 tbsp (15 mL) cornstarch

¼ cup (60 mL) sugar

¼ cup (60 mL) white vinegar

¼ cup (60 mL) catsup

¼ cup (60 mL) pickle juice

1½ cups (375 mL) oil, for deep-frying

1 Combine pork, salt, flour, sherry and egg yolk in a bowl. Let stand 15 minutes. Roll pork pieces in cornstarch just before deep-frying.

2 Heat oil in a saucepan. Add ginger and garlic, and stir-fry 30 seconds. Add pickles and green and red peppers. Blend water, cornstarch, sugar, vinegar, catsup and pickle juice. Stir into vegetables until mixture thickens. Keep warm.

3 Heat deep-frying oil. Cook pork in four batches for 5 minutes each. Remove and drain.

4 Reheat oil, refry pork 3–5 minutes. Drain well. Arrange on a serving platter. Spoon sauce on top and serve at once.

SERVES 6

BRAISED NORTHERN LAMB

1 lb (450 g) boneless lamb
¼ cup (60 mL) soy sauce
¼ cup (60 mL) dry sherry
1 tbsp (15 mL) sugar
1 tsp (5 mL) five-spice powder
3 tbsp (45 mL) vegetable oil
1 tsp (5 mL) chopped garlic
1 tsp (5 mL) chopped fresh ginger
1 medium onion, cut in ¾ inch (2 cm) cubes
1 tsp (5 mL) Szechuan peppercorns, ground
2 cups (500 mL) stock
3 potatoes, peeled and cut in 1 inch (2.5 cm) cubes

1 Combine lamb, soy sauce, sherry, sugar and five-spice powder. Marinate 1 hour. Turn lamb pieces occasionally. Drain lamb, reserving marinade.

2 Heat oil in a pan. Add lamb and fry until golden and sealed on all sides.

3 Add garlic, ginger, onion and peppercorns. Stir-fry 2 minutes. Add reserved marinade and stock to cover. Bring to a boil. Simmer covered 1½ hours.

4 Add diced potatoes, and continue cooking 30 minutes or until tender.

SERVES 6

CHAR SUI

1⅔ lbs (750 g) boneless pork
1½ tbsp (20 mL) honey combined with 1½ tbsp (20 mL) hot water

MARINADE

3 tbsp (45 mL) soy sauce
2 tbsp (30 mL) dry sherry
¼ cup (60 mL) hoisin sauce
1 tsp (5 mL) five-spice powder
1 tsp (5 mL) sesame paste
1 tsp (5 mL) brown sugar
1 slice fresh ginger
1 clove garlic, crushed
3 tbsp (45 mL) vegetable oil
dash red food coloring

1 **TO MAKE MARINADE:** Combine marinade ingredients in bowl.

2 Cut pork into strips 1¼ x 6 inches (3 x 15 cm). Pierce all over with a skewer. Add to marinade, stirring to coat. Let stand 1 hour or overnight in refrigerator.

3 Roast pork Chinese style on a rack over a pan of water (see page 6), at 400°F (200°C) for 15 minutes. Baste with marinade. Reduce heat to 350°F (180°C). Roast a further 10 minutes.

4 Brush pork with honey mixture on each side, and continue cooking for 10 minutes.

5 Slice pork thinly. Serve hot or cold or in combination recipes.

SERVES 4–6

❖ **MARINATING**

Marinate foods overnight for tenderness and flavor.

POULTRY

Duck and chicken are favorite fare in China and the Chinese have created many interesting ways of preparing them. Drying, smoking and curing are methods used with duck as well as roasting, simmering, steaming and, of course, stir-frying. Many of the same methods are used for chicken.

Whole chickens from Chinese specialty shops often come complete with head and feet. The reason for this is that the beak and feet give an indication as to the age of a chicken – they should be pliable. Simply cut the neck and feet off and use in the stock pot.

If using a frozen chicken, make sure it is completely defrosted before cooking. It will take up to 24 hours to defrost a whole chicken in the refrigerator.

When using fresh duck, make sure the oil sacs in the tail have been removed before cooking. Ducks are sometimes trussed and immersed in boiling water to remove the excess oil that, as water birds, they have under their skin. Always pierce the skin of a whole duck in several places before cooking.

*Shanghai-style Chicken and
Five-spice Chicken (page 50)*

SHANGHAI-STYLE CHICKEN

1 medium onion, peeled and chopped

1 carrot, peeled and chopped

1 stalk celery, chopped

6 fresh parsley stalks

1 slice fresh ginger

1 tsp (5 mL) white peppercorns

2 bay leaves

6 cups (1.5 L) cold water

3 lb (1.5 kg) chicken

1 lb (450 g) fresh green asparagus

3 tbsp (45 mL) toasted sesame seeds,
to sprinkle

SAUCE

3 tbsp (45 mL) vegetable oil

1 onion, peeled and thinly sliced

½ tsp (2.5 mL) chopped garlic

2 red chili peppers, seeded and chopped

1 tbsp (15 mL) oyster sauce

1 tbsp (15 mL) soy sauce

1 cup (250 mL) chicken stock

salt and pepper

1 tbsp (15 mL) cornstarch

1 Cook chicken by placing onion, carrot, celery, seasonings and water into a large saucepan. Bring to a boil, add chicken and simmer until tender. Remove chicken meat from carcass in strips. Set aside.

2 Snap off tough ends of asparagus stalks. Scrape stems lightly with a peeler or small sharp knife. Wash well.

3 Tie asparagus in several bunches. Cook in boiling salted water 6–8 minutes. Refresh in cold water.

4 TO MAKE SAUCE: Heat oil in a saucepan. Sauté onion and garlic 2–3 minutes and add chili peppers. Blend oyster sauce, soy sauce, stock, salt, pepper and cornstarch together. Add to onion mixture and stir until boiling.

5 Arrange cooked asparagus on a serving platter. Top with chicken strips. Spoon sauce over chicken and sprinkle with sesame seeds. Serve hot.

QUICK VARIATION: Use canned asparagus spears. Cook chicken in a microwave on HIGH (100%) for 27 minutes. Prepare sauce while chicken is cooking.

SERVES 6–8

❖ HINT

When cooking, add ingredients which require longest cooking times to pan or wok first.

FIVE-SPICE CHICKEN

3 lb (1.5 kg) chicken

4 green onions, shredded

MARINADE

1 tsp (5 mL) chopped garlic

¼ cup (60 mL) soy sauce

3 tbsp (45 mL) vegetable oil

½ tsp (2.5 mL) five-spice powder

½ tsp (2.5 mL) sugar

1 Combine marinade ingredients. Brush mixture inside and over chicken. Let stand 30 minutes on a rack over a pan of water.

2 Drain chicken and roast Chinese style (see page 6) at 350°F (180°C) until tender. Baste and turn chicken four times during cooking for even browning.

3 Chop chicken Chinese style (see facing page). Serve hot garnished with green onions.

QUICK VARIATION: Place drained chicken in a glass dish on a microwave roasting rack. Cook uncovered 27 minutes on HIGH (100%), turning and basting every 10 minutes.

SERVES 6–8

STEP-BY-STEP TECHNIQUES

1 *Remove leg and thigh by cutting lengthwise between thigh and breast.*

2 *Halve chicken by cutting along the backbone from the tail to the neck.*

3 *Remove wings and separate drumsticks from thighs at the joint.*

4 *Divide wings into two pieces at the joints, and chop drumsticks and thighs into three pieces each. Slice breasts into three or four pieces depending on the size of the chicken.*

CRISP SPICED CHICKEN

3 lb (1.5 kg) chicken

1 tsp (5 mL) five-spice powder

1 tbsp (15 mL) cornstarch

oil, for deep-frying

lemon wedges and green onions, to serve

1 Wash and clean chicken. Dry thoroughly and chop through the bone into 10 or 12 pieces (see technique above). Combine five-spice powder and cornstarch and toss with chicken.

2 Heat oil in a wok and deep-fry chicken pieces in batches for 5 minutes each batch; drain well. Reheat the oil and deep-fry chicken until golden brown and cooked. Drain on paper towels.

3 Serve hot with rice, lemon wedges and green onions.

NOTE: If you find five-spice powder very pungent, reduce the quantity to ½ tsp (2.5 mL) the first time you make the dish.

SERVES 4

HONEY LEMON CHICKEN

2 lbs (1 kg) fresh chicken pieces

3 tbsp (45 mL) soy sauce

1 tbsp (15 mL) dry sherry

juice of 2 lemons, strained

3–4 tbsp (45-60 mL) honey

3 tbsp (45 mL) vegetable oil

1 tsp (5 mL) chopped fresh ginger

1 tsp (5 mL) chopped garlic

¼ tsp (1 mL) salt

1½ cups (375 mL) chicken stock or water

**1½ tbsp (20 mL) cornstarch blended with
3 tbsp (45 mL) cold water**

slices of fresh lemon, to serve

*Smoked Chicken and
Braised Chicken with
Peking Sauce*

1   Pierce chicken pieces with a skewer. Combine soy sauce, sherry, lemon juice and honey. Brush over chicken pieces and let stand 30 minutes.

2   Heat oil. Add ginger, garlic and salt. Add drained chicken pieces and brown evenly. Pour off excess oil, add marinade and stock. Simmer covered 45 minutes until tender. Turn chicken pieces twice during cooking. Remove chicken and place on a serving platter. Stir blended cornstarch and water into sauce and bring to boil. Strain sauce and spoon over chicken pieces. Serve with lemon slices.

SERVES 6

BRAISED CHICKEN WITH PEKING SAUCE

1 lb (450 g) boned chicken breast, sliced

½ tsp (2.5 mL) salt

1 egg white, beaten

1½ cups (375 mL) vegetable oil

1 clove garlic, crushed

1 slice fresh ginger

1 tbsp (15 mL) vegetable oil

2 onions, cut in eighths

1 red pepper, cut in ¾ inch (2 cm) cubes

3 tbsp (45 mL) hoisin sauce

1 tbsp (15 mL) dry sherry

2 oz (60 g) vermicelli noodles

1 Mix chicken slices with salt and egg white. Heat oil. Add garlic and ginger, remove when brown. Deep-fry chicken pieces in oil until white. Drain well on paper towels.

2 Heat 1 tbsp (15 mL) oil. Add onions and red pepper, stir-fry 2 minutes. Stir in hoisin sauce, sherry and chicken to reheat.

3 Cut noodles into 2 inch (5 cm) lengths. Deep-fry in hot oil until they puff up. Drain well on paper towels. Arrange on a serving platter and top with chicken mixture.

SERVES 6

SMOKED CHICKEN

3 lb (1.5 kg) chicken

3 tbsp (45 mL) brown peppercorns

1 tbsp (15 mL) salt

8 cups (2 L) water

4 green onions

3 slices fresh ginger

2 whole star anise

1 cinnamon stick

1 cup (250 mL) soy sauce

½ cup (125 mL) sugar

½ cup (125 mL) all-purpose flour

½ cup (125 mL) dry tea leaves

1 tbsp (15 mL) sesame oil

1 Clean and wipe chicken. Fry peppercorns and salt for 1 minute in a wok. Rub into chicken and allow to stand for 2 hours.

2 Bring water to a boil in a large pan. Add green onions, ginger, star anise, cinnamon and soy sauce and simmer 10 minutes. Add chicken and cook for 10 minutes over low heat, turning once. Remove chicken and allow to cool.

3 Put sugar, flour and tea leaves in a wok, and cover with a rack. Sit chicken on its side on rack. Cover tightly and smoke for 45 minutes – 1 hour, over a low heat, turning chicken halfway through. Remove chicken from wok and brush with sesame oil; cool.

4 Chop Chinese style (page 51) and arrange on a platter.

SERVES 6

SWEET AND SOUR SESAME CHICKEN

3 lb (1.5 kg) chicken, cut up

¼ cup (60 mL) plum sauce

1 tbsp (15 mL) vinegar

2 cups (500 mL) chicken stock

⅓ cup (85 mL) dry sherry

1 tbsp (15 mL) finely chopped fresh ginger

1 onion, quartered

6 oz (180 g) canned straw mushrooms

2 stalks celery, sliced

8 oz (225 g) canned water chestnuts

8 oz (225 g) canned bamboo shoots, drained and sliced

3 tbsp (45 mL) cornstarch blended with water

1 tbsp (15 mL) sesame seeds

1 Preheat oven to 350°F (180°C). Arrange chicken in an ovenproof dish. Combine plum sauce, vinegar, stock, sherry and ginger and pour over chicken. Cover and bake 40 minutes.

2 Add vegetables, return to oven and cook a further 15 minutes. Remove chicken and vegetables to a heated serving dish.

3 Thicken remaining liquid with blended cornstarch and water. Bring to a boil and simmer 2 minutes. Pour over chicken. Sprinkle with sesame seeds and serve hot with rice.

SERVES 6

❖ **HINT**

Toast sesame seeds in a dry pan and store in a jar. Keep a stock of oven-roasted nuts to use as a garnish

PEKING DOILIES

1¼ cups (310 mL) water

2 cups (500 mL) all-purpose flour, sifted

oil or sesame oil, or a combination of the two

1 In a pan, bring water to a boil. Add flour, all at once, and stir very quickly with a wooden spoon to combine. Remove from pan and knead mixture on a floured board until smooth, about 10 minutes. Cover with a damp towel and let stand for 10 minutes.

2 Form the dough into a long roll 1¼ inch (3 cm) in diameter. Cut into ½ inch (1 cm) thick slices. Flatten to ¼ inch (0.5 cm) thickness and brush one side of half the rounds with a little oil. Place one unoiled round on top of the oiled side of another. Dust each pair with flour and roll out to a very thin pancake, about 4–5 inches (10–12 cm) in diameter. Roll from the center, turning the pancake a little after each roll to ensure a perfect circle of even thickness.

3 Heat an ungreased wok or griddle over low to medium heat. Bake one pancake at a time for about 1 minute on each side or until lightly colored.

4 Transfer to a platter, separate the two halves and keep covered with a towel until all pancakes are ready. Peking doilies can be made in advance, kept in the refrigerator and reheated by steaming for 8–10 minutes.

MAKES 15–25 DOILIES
(DEPENDING ON THICKNESS)

PEKING DUCK

4½ lb (2 kg) duck

½–¾ cup (125–185 mL) water

5 tbsp (75 mL) honey

Peking doilies

green onion curls

½ cucumber

½–¾ cup (125–185 mL) hoisin sauce or plum sauce

❖ **PEKING DUCK**

Sometimes only the skin is eaten and the meat used as an ingredient for other dishes.

1 Choose a fresh duck with neck and skin intact. Wash duck, immerse in boiling water, lift out and dry thoroughly inside and out. Hang duck overnight in a cool airy place, to allow the skin to dry thoroughly.

2 Dissolve honey in water and brush skin until completely saturated with honey. Hang duck to dry completely for about 6 hours or until the skin is dry and slightly hardened by the honey.

3 Meanwhile, prepare Peking doilies and green onion curls. Peel cucumber and cut in half lengthwise. Scoop out the seedy center part and cut into strips.

4 To separate the skin from the flesh of the duck, insert a straw immediately underneath the skin and blow through it. Place duck on a rack over a drip pan. Roast in a 350°F (180°C) oven without basting for 1½–2 hours or until skin is browned and crisp.

5 With a very sharp knife, slice off skin and cut into squares. Carve meat in thick slices and serve separately during the meal. Take a doily and top with one or two pieces of skin, green onion curls, cucumber strips and hoisin sauce. Roll doily to eat.

SERVES 6

EIGHT JEWEL DUCK

4½ lb (2 kg) boned duck

salt

1 cup (250 mL) uncooked rice

1 tbsp (15 mL) vegetable oil

½ tsp (2.5 mL) chopped fresh ginger

½ tsp (2.5 mL) chopped garlic

¼ lb (110 g) ground pork

4 Chinese mushrooms, soaked in warm water 20 minutes

2 oz (60 g) bamboo shoots

6 water chestnuts

4 uncooked or 10 dried shrimp, soaked and diced

2 thin slices ham, diced

¼ cup (60 mL) toasted almonds, chopped

1 tbsp (15 mL) soy sauce

1 tbsp (15 mL) dry sherry

1 green onion

1 Lightly salt duck inside and out. Cook rice using Chinese Rice recipe (page 84). Cut all vegetables into small dice.

2 Heat a wok. Add oil, ginger, garlic and pork. Stir-fry 4 minutes. Add mushrooms, bamboo shoots, chestnuts, shrimp, ham and almonds. Stir-fry until hot. Add soy sauce, sherry and green onion. Fold in rice. Allow mixture to cool.

3 Pack mixture into cavity of duck. Secure openings with poultry skewers. Reshape duck and brush lightly with oil. Place a

sheet of foil on top of a cake rack over a baking dish containing 1¼ inches (3 cm) cold water.

4 Arrange duck breast side up on foil. Roast at 400°F (200°C) for 30 minutes. Reduce heat to 350°F (180°C) and cook 1–1½ hours until duck is golden and tender. Turn duck occasionally for even browning.

5 Remove skewers and carve. Serve hot or cold.

SERVES 8

Peking Duck served with Peking Doilies

*Roast Duck
and Plum Sauce*

❖ **HINT**

*To plump ducks, place
fresh ducks in boiling
water to cover. Allow to
stand 5 minutes. This
firms the duck flesh before
roasting or steaming.
Drain well, then follow
recipe instructions.*

ROAST DUCK
AND
PLUM SAUCE

4½–5½ lb (2–2.5 kg) duck

1 tbsp (15 mL) vegetable oil

¼ cup (60 mL) plum sauce

MARINADE

¼ cup (60 mL) chicken stock

1 tbsp (15 mL) brown sugar

3 tbsp (45 mL) soy sauce

2 tbsp (30 mL) honey

1 tsp (5 mL) five-spice powder

1 Combine marinade ingredients in a large bowl. Add duck and baste with mixture. Marinate 1 hour. Baste and turn duck every 15 minutes.

2 Drain duck, reserving marinade. Roast duck Chinese style on a rack over a pan of water (see page 6) at 350°F (180°C) for 2 hours, basting with marinade every 30 minutes.

3 Chop duck into serving pieces and arrange on a serving platter. Heat oil in a saucepan, add plum sauce and heat through. Pour over duck.

SERVES 6–8

STIR-FRIED DUCK AND BITTER MELON

1 tbsp (15 mL) fermented black beans

1 clove garlic

4½ lb (2 kg) duck

1 tbsp (15 mL) hoisin sauce

1 tbsp (15 mL) sherry

½ tsp (2.5 mL) chili pepper sauce

1 tbsp (15 mL) cornstarch

½ lb (225 g) fresh or canned bitter melon

5 tbsp (75 mL) oil

1 cup (250 mL) chicken stock

extra 2 tsp (10 mL) cornstarch

3 tbsp (45 mL) water

1 Soak black beans in water for 10 minutes. Drain and mash beans with garlic. Cut duck meat from breast and legs and reserve carcass for making stock. Cut meat across the grain into ½ inch (1 cm) thick slices.

2 Mix hoisin sauce, sherry, chili pepper sauce and cornstarch. Add duck slices and mix well. Marinate for 20 minutes. If using fresh bitter melon, wash and drain. Remove stalks, halve bitter melon lengthwise and remove seedy center. Cut into thin slices. Bring plenty of salted water to boil, add bitter melon and parboil 4 minutes.

3 Rinse under cold running water until completely cooled; drain. If using canned bitter melon, drain liquid, rinse under cold running water, drain and slice.

4 Heat half the oil in a wok. Add black bean mixture and stir-fry for 30 seconds. Add duck slices and stir-fry until lightly colored. Remove and keep warm. Add remaining oil, heat and stir-fry the bitter melon for 1–1½ minutes. Add stock and bring to a boil. Return duck slices to wok, reduce heat, cover and simmer until heated through. Blend cornstarch with water and add to wok; cook until sauce is thickened.

SERVES 4–6

DEEP-FRIED DUCK IN LYCHEE SAUCE

3½–4½ lb (1.5–2 kg) fresh duck

2 eggs

¾ cup (185 mL) all-purpose flour

3 tbsp (45 mL) ginger wine

½ tsp (2.5 mL) salt

1½ cups (375 mL) vegetable oil, for deep-frying

LYCHEE SAUCE

1 tbsp (15 mL) vegetable oil

½ tsp (2.5 mL) chopped garlic

½ red pepper, cut in ¾ inch (2 cm) cubes

½ green pepper, cut in ¾ inch (2 cm) cubes

7 oz (200 g) canned lychee fruit

½ cup (125 mL) lychee juice

1/4 cup (60 mL) water

½ cup (125 mL) white vinegar

⅓ cup (85 mL) sugar

1 tbsp (15 mL) catsup

1½ tbsp (20 mL) cornstarch blended with 3 tbsp (45 mL) water

1 Cut duck meat into 1 inch (2.5 cm) pieces, leaving skin on. Beat eggs, blend in flour, wine and salt to form a batter. Add duck pieces and stir to coat.

2 Heat oil, add duck in batter six pieces at a time. Cook until golden. Drain well and keep warm on a serving platter. To make sauce, heat oil in a wok. Add garlic, green and red peppers and lychees. Stir-fry 1 minute. Remove from pan.

3 Stir in lychee juice, water, vinegar, sugar and catsup. Bring to a boil. Stir in combined cornstarch and water. When boiling, return vegetables and lychee fruit to reheat. Spoon over duck cubes.

SERVES 6

❖ **TOASTING RAW NUTS**

Add nuts to boiling water to cover. Cook 3–5 minutes. This softens nuts to the center. Drain and dry.

Heat enough oil to cover nuts. Add nuts and toast them until they turn a pale ivory color, stirring during cooking. Drain well and cool before using. Nuts will be crisp and cooked to the center.

HEALTHY
VEGETARIAN FARE

One of the most remarkable aspects of Chinese cooking is the approach to vegetables. They are of the utmost importance. This emphasis is due partly to the influence of Buddhist monks, who established strict vegetarian rules. Small wonder this resulted in the development of extraordinary skill in preparing vegetables.

The main difference between the Chinese method of cooking vegetables and the Western way is that in the Chinese way, vegetables are cooked only long enough to bring out all their qualities of crispness, tenderness and brightness of color. The vegetables are served at the peak of their flavor. This does not mean that they are served raw; even in salads, the vegetables will usually be cooked briefly.

Cutting is of the utmost importance in the preparation of vegetables. Vegetables are cut, blanched and parboiled in such a way that the final cooking can be completed at one time, even though the textures of the individual vegetables differ greatly. The soft leafy vegetables require less cooking than the tougher ones.

*Noodle Soup with Quail Eggs, Stir-fried Bean Curd
with Szechuan Sauce and Bean Sprout Salad (page 60)*

NOODLE SOUP WITH QUAIL EGGS

4–6 cups (1–1.5 L) water

½ lb (225 g) fresh egg noodles

¾ tsp (3 mL) salt

2 tsp (10 mL) soy sauce

1 tsp (5 mL) peanut oil

few drops sesame oil

pinch white pepper

12 quail eggs, boiled and shelled

3 green onions, finely cut

8 cups (2 L) boiling vegetable stock

1 Bring water to a boil. Add salt and noodles. Cook 3–5 minutes until just tender. Drain, then rinse in cold water. Drain again.

2 Place noodles in a large tureen. Add soy sauce, peanut and sesame oils and pepper. Toss well to mix.

3 Arrange eggs and green onions over noodles. Pour over stock and serve at once with the sauce of your choice. Quail eggs taste particularly delicious with Szechuan Sauce.

SERVES 6

SZECHUAN SAUCE

3 tbsp (45 mL) vegetable oil

3 red chili peppers, chopped

2 tsp (10 mL) chopped ginger

2 tsp (10 mL) chopped garlic

½ medium onion, chopped

3 tbsp (45 mL) dry sherry

5 tbsp (75 mL) sugar

5 tbsp (75 mL) catsup

5 tbsp (75 mL) white vinegar

1 Heat oil in a pan. Add chili peppers, ginger, garlic and onion. Fry until tender.

2 Add sherry, sugar, catsup and vinegar, and simmer 10–15 minutes.

MAKES APPROXIMATELY 1 CUP (250 ML)

STIR-FRIED BEAN CURD WITH SZECHUAN SAUCE

¼ cup (60 mL) vegetable oil

¼ tsp (1 mL) salt

2 green onions, cut in ¾ inch (2 cm) lengths

1 lb (450 g) firm bean curd, cut in ¾ inch (2 cm) cubes

5 tbsp (75 mL) Szechuan Sauce

1 Heat oil in a wok. Add salt, white of green onions and bean curd cubes. Stir-fry gently to heat through.

2 Add Szechuan Sauce and simmer 3 minutes. Stir in green onion tops and serve.

SERVES 6–8

BEAN SPROUT SALAD

1 lb (450 g) soybean sprouts

3 tbsp (45 mL) light soy sauce

1 tbsp (15 mL) white vinegar

1 tsp (5 mL) sugar

½ tsp (2.5 mL) sesame oil

½ lb (225 g) snow peas

1 bean curd cake, cut in julienne strips

¼ red pepper, cut in julienne strips

1 Blanch soybean sprouts in boiling water for 1 minute. Refresh in cold water and drain well.

2 Combine soy sauce, vinegar, sugar and sesame oil in a bowl, add soybean sprouts and snow peas. Toss to coat with dressing. Cover and chill 20 minutes.

3 Arrange salad on a platter. Garnish with bean curd and red pepper.

SERVES 8

STEP-BY-STEP TECHNIQUES

1 *Cut bean curd cakes in half.*
Make a pocket in each half to contain filling.

2 *Carefully stuff cakes with filling.*

3 *Place cakes on a shallow heatproof plate and steam for about 25 minutes.*

STUFFED BEAN CURD

6 cakes bean curd

2 tbsp (30 mL) oil

1 thin slice fresh ginger, finely chopped

1 clove garlic, crushed

**2 stalks celery, or 6 leaves cabbage
or other seasonal green vegetable, cut into
1½ inch (4 cm) diamonds**

¾ cup (185 mL) chicken stock

3 tbsp (45 mL) soy sauce

1 tbsp (15 mL) sherry

**1½ tbsp (20 mL) cornstarch blended
with 3 tbsp (45 mL) water**

FILLING

½ lb (225 g) tempeh, grated

6 green onions, minced

2 water chestnuts, minced

2 tsp (10 mL) soy sauce

1 tbsp (15 mL) sherry

1 egg yolk

1 Cut bean curd cakes in half. Make a pocket in each half to contain filling, taking care not to break bean curd. In a bowl, combine filling ingredients. Stuff bean curd carefully with this mixture. Place bean curd in a shallow heatproof dish and steam for about 25 minutes.

2 About 5 minutes before the steaming is completed, heat oil in a wok. Add ginger and garlic. Stir-fry 1 minute until golden brown. Discard ginger and garlic. Increase heat, add celery and stir-fry for 1 minute. Add chicken stock, soy sauce and sherry.

3 Reduce heat, cover and continue cooking for 1½ minutes. Stir blended cornstarch and water into vegetables. Cook 30 seconds until thickened. Remove dish with bean curd from the steamer. Serve with vegetable sauce and rice.

SERVES 4

Braised Vegetables

2 Heat oil in a wok. Add garlic and ginger, and stir for 1 minute. Add vegetables and bamboo shoots and stir-fry over high heat about 2 minutes. Add vinegar, sugar, sherry and chicken stock and bring to a boil. Stir in blended cornstarch and water to thicken.

SERVES 4

ASPARAGUS IN THE SNOW

1 lb (450 g) fresh green asparagus, tough ends removed

1 slice fresh ginger

1 tbsp (15 mL) dry sherry

3 tbsp (45 mL) vegetable stock

2 egg whites

1 tbsp (15 mL) cornstarch

1 cup (250 mL) seasoned vegetable stock

1 Place asparagus, ginger, sherry and stock into pan. Cook over high heat 3–4 minutes until crispy tender. Place asparagus on a serving platter, reserving cooking liquid.
2 To make sauce, beat egg whites with asparagus cooking liquid. Blend cornstarch with seasoned stock. Heat until thickened. Whisk 3 tbsp (45 mL) heated thickened stock into egg mixture. Whisk egg mixture into remaining stock. Serve hot.

SERVES 4

SWEET AND SOUR VEGETABLES

1 green pepper

1 medium onion

2 stalks celery

2 carrots

3 tbsp (45 mL) oil

1 clove garlic, crushed

2 thin slices fresh ginger, finely chopped

2 oz (60 g) canned bamboo shoots, shredded

¼ cup (60 mL) vinegar

3 tbsp (45 mL) sugar

1 tbsp (15 mL) sherry

3 tbsp (45 mL) chicken stock

1½ tbsp (20 mL) cornstarch blended with 3 tbsp (45 mL) water

1 Remove membrane and seeds from green pepper and cut into 2 inch (5 cm) long diamond shapes. Peel onion, halve lengthwise and cut each half into ½ inch (1 cm) wide strips lengthwise. Cut celery in 2 inch (5 cm) pieces diagonally. Cut carrots diagonally into 1½ inch (4 cm) pieces. Parboil vegetables for 3–4 minutes.

BRAISED VEGETABLES

3 tbsp (45 mL) oil

1 tsp (5 mL) sesame oil

1 clove garlic, crushed

1 tsp (5 mL) finely chopped fresh ginger

1 lb (450 g) prepared mixed vegetables of your choice

½ cup (125 mL) hot water

1 tbsp (15 mL) oyster sauce

1 tbsp (15 mL) soy sauce

2 tsp (10 mL) cornstarch blended with 1½ tbsp (20 mL) water

1 In a wok heat oil and add sesame oil, garlic and ginger. Add vegetables and stir-fry 2 minutes. Add hot water, oyster and soy sauces. Simmer 4 minutes.

2 Push vegetables to one side of wok, add combined cornstarch and water and stir until sauce thickens. Toss vegetables through sauce and serve with boiled rice.

SERVES 4

STIR-FRIED BROCCOLI AND BEAN CURD IN OYSTER SAUCE

1 lb (450 g) broccoli

3 tbsp (45 mL) oil

fresh ginger, sliced

1 clove garlic, finely chopped

¼ cup (60 mL) canned bamboo shoots, shredded

2 cakes bean curd, cut in ½ inch (1 cm) cubes

3 tbsp (45 mL) oyster sauce

1 tbsp (15 mL) soy sauce

½ cup (125 mL) chicken stock

1 tsp (5 mL) cornstarch blended with 3 tbsp (45 mL) water

1 Cut off florets from broccoli stems. Discard tough ends and cut wide stems in half lengthwise. Cut in ¾ inch (2 cm) pieces diagonally. Parboil broccoli in a large quantity of salted water 3–4 minutes. Drain and rinse broccoli under cold running water. Cool completely.

2 Heat oil in a wok until very hot. Add ginger and garlic. Stir-fry 1 minute until ginger is lightly browned. Discard ginger and garlic. Add drained broccoli and stir-fry 1 minute. Add bamboo shoots, bean curd, sauces and chicken stock. Bring to a boil, reduce heat, cover and simmer for 2 minutes. Stir in blended cornstarch and water to thicken the sauce.

SERVES 4

STIR-FRIED BEAN SPROUTS

¾ lb (340 g) bean sprouts

3 tbsp (45 mL) oil

1 thin slice fresh ginger, finely chopped

½ green pepper, sliced

½ medium onion, cut in wedges

12 green onions, sliced

2 thin slices ham, shredded

3 tbsp (45 mL) chicken stock combined with 2 tsp (10 mL) sherry

1 Pour boiling water over bean sprouts and let stand 20 seconds.

2 Refresh in cold running water, drain and dry. Heat oil in a wok. Add ginger and stir-fry 30 seconds. Add green pepper, onion and green onions and stir-fry 1½ minutes.

Add bean sprouts and ham and stir-fry 30 seconds. Add combined stock and sherry and bring to a boil. Remove from heat and serve.

SERVES 4

Stir-fried Broccoli and Bean Curd in Oyster Sauce

*Mock Duck Foo Yung
and Crunchy Omelet
in a Nest*

salt and pepper

1 tbsp (15 mL) light soy sauce

2 oz (60 g) vermicelli noodles,
fried and lightly crushed

1 green onion, shredded

1 Heat oil in a pan. Add onion and stir-fry with mock duck, peas and corn 2 minutes. Stir in eggs, salt, pepper and soy sauce. Draw edges of mixture into the center until set, without allowing mixture to dry.

2 Place noodles on a serving platter. Place egg mixture on top, leaving a noodle border. Top with green onion shreds.

SERVES 8

VEGETABLE CHOW MEIN

1½ cups (375 mL) vegetable oil

½ lb (225 g) fresh noodles

3 tbsp (45 mL) vegetable oil

½ tsp (2.5 mL) chopped garlic

1 small onion, shredded

1 medium carrot, sliced and parboiled

⅓ lb (150 g) bamboo shoots, sliced

5 oz (150 g) mini corn

8 fresh mushrooms, thickly sliced

½ lb (225 g) fresh mustard cabbage
(choy sum), cut into 1 inch (2.5 cm) lengths

1 tbsp (15 mL) soy sauce

½ cup (125 mL) vegetable stock

1½ tbsp (20 mL) cornstarch blended with
¼ cup (60 mL) vegetable stock

1 Heat oil in a pan. Add one-third of the noodles. Fry until crisp, turning over with tongs during cooking. Drain well and repeat until all noodles are cooked. Set aside on a warm serving platter.

2 Heat 3 tbsp (45 mL) oil. Add garlic, onion, carrot, bamboo shoots and corn. Stir-fry 1 minute. Add mushrooms, cabbage, soy sauce and stock. Cook covered 2 minutes.

3 Stir in blended cornstarch and stock to thicken. Serve hot over fried noodles.

SERVES 4–6

MOCK DUCK FOO YUNG

3 tbsp (45 mL) vegetable oil

1 medium onion, shredded

10 oz (280 g) can vegetarian mock
duck, thinly sliced

⅓ cup (85 mL) green peas, blanched

⅓ cup (85 mL) corn kernels,
canned or cooked

6 eggs, beaten

STEAMED DIM SUM

24 wonton wrappers

lettuce leaf, for steaming

FILLING

½ lb (225 g) firm bean curd, finely chopped

¼ lb (110 g) soybeans, cooked and mashed

1 green onion, finely chopped

1 tbsp (15 mL) chopped fresh coriander leaves

3 tbsp (45 mL) celery, finely chopped

2 Chinese mushrooms, soaked in warm water 20 minutes and chopped

2 tsp (10 mL) soy sauce

¼ tsp (1 mL) sesame oil

salt and pepper

1 Combine all filling ingredients. Place 2 tsp (10 mL) filling onto each wonton wrapper. Gather outer edges of skin around filling in a cup shape. Press gently so that filling rises to the top of wrapper. The base should be flat.

2 Place a lettuce leaf in steamer. Arrange dim sum on top, leaving space between each to prevent sticking.

3 Steam 10 minutes. Serve with soy vinegar dip.

MAKES 24 DIM SUM

CRUNCHY OMELET IN A NEST

3 tbsp (45 mL) vegetable oil

1 medium onion, finely shredded

2 stalks celery, finely chopped

½ red pepper, finely chopped

5 fresh mushrooms, thickly sliced

¼ lb (110 g) bean sprouts, root removed

salt and pepper

6 eggs, beaten

1 green onion, finely chopped

1 tbsp (15 mL) chopped cashew nuts

1 large potato nest (see page 80)

1 Heat oil in a wok. Add onion, celery and red pepper, and stir-fry 2 minutes. Add mushrooms, bean sprouts and seasonings

and stir-fry 1 minute. Pour in eggs. Fold into vegetables until mixture sets. Turn over and cook for 1 minute.

2 Remove and cut into strips. Place into potato nest. Sprinkle with green onions and cashews, and serve at once.

SERVES 4–6

BEAN CURD OMELET

3 tbsp (45 mL) vegetable oil

¼ tsp (1 mL) salt

2 green onions, finely chopped

⅓ cup (85 mL) peas, blanched in boiling water 1 minute

¼ lb (110 g) bean curd, cut in ½ inch (1 cm) dice

6 eggs, beaten

1 tbsp (15 mL) light soy sauce

1 Heat oil in a wok. Add salt, green onions, peas and bean curd. Stir-fry 1 minute.

2 Pour in eggs. Cook over medium heat until mixture begins to set. Draw outer edges to the center until eggs are the consistency of scrambled eggs, moist and retaining shape.

3 Sprinkle with soy sauce before serving.

SERVES 4–6

BARBECUED BEAN CURD

½ lb (225 g) firm bean curd

¼ cup (60 mL) char sui marinade (page 47)

1 Pierce bean curd with toothpick. Coat evenly with char sui sauce and marinate 30 minutes.

2 The bean curd can be oven-roasted Chinese style (see page 6) for 20 minutes at 350°F (180°C) or pan-fried in 4–5 tbsp (60–75 mL) oil, turning to cook each side.

3 Cool and slice. Use for stir-fry combinations, soups or in fried rice.

MAKES ½ LB (225 G)

❖ **HINT**

Instant noodles are available both plain and flavored with chicken, shrimp, beef, curry or vegetables. They can be used in soups, or stir-fried with a topping. Their cooking time of 2 minutes has captured the noodle market. Dried noodles can be boiled then mixed with a small amount of oil and refrigerated in portion sizes several days before use.

STIR-FRIED HONEY DUCK

10 oz (280 g) can vegetarian mock duck

2 tsp (10 mL) vegetable oil

½ tsp (2.5 mL) chopped garlic

2 green onions, sliced

2 tbsp (30 mL) light soy sauce

2 tbsp (30 mL) dry sherry

1 tbsp (15 mL) honey

1 tsp (5 mL) cornstarch blended with 2 tsp (10 mL) stock

1 Cut mock duck into even-sized ¾–1 inch (2–2.5 cm) pieces.

2 Heat oil in a pan. Add garlic and green onions and stir-fry 1 minute. Add soy sauce, sherry and honey, simmer 2 minutes. Add vegetarian duck pieces and simmer 15 minutes. Thicken with blended cornstarch and stock and serve.

SERVES 4

❖ **MOCK DUCK**

First made in China in the tenth century AD, mock duck is made from wheat flour gluten, safflower oil, soybean extract, sugar, salt and water. Considered a delicacy, it is available canned, and can be used to replace real duck in most recipes.

BEAN CURD AND POTATO ROLLS

½ lb (225 g) boiled potatoes, mashed

½ lb (225 g) firm bean curd, mashed and drained

2 green onions, finely chopped

salt and pepper

2 large spring roll wrappers

cold water or egg white

oil, for deep-frying

1 Combine potato, bean curd, green onions, and salt and pepper in a bowl. Halve mixture and shape each half into a roll, 4 inches (10 cm) long.

2 Arrange spring roll wrappers with one corner towards you. Brush edges with cold water or egg white. Place one roll crosswise on each skin. Fold lowest point of skin over filling and roll once. Fold left and right points into center. Brush edges again. Roll up firmly to cook.

3 Fry in oil to cover until golden and crisp.

4 To cook using the oven method, place rolls on greased baking sheet, brush with oil and bake at 400°F (200°C) for 20 minutes until golden.

SERVES 4–6

VEGETABLE SPRING ROLLS

3 tbsp (45 mL) vegetable oil

6 medium Chinese mushrooms, soaked in warm water 20 minutes and sliced

2 medium onions, sliced

½ tsp (2.5 mL) chopped garlic

1 tsp (5 mL) chopped fresh ginger

⅔ lb (300 g) Chinese cabbage, shredded

1 cup (250 mL) celery, sliced

1 cup (250 mL) green beans, sliced

1 cup (250 mL) carrot, grated

2 oz (60 g) soybean sprouts

¼ lb (110 g) water chestnuts

¼ cup (60 mL) light soy sauce

1 tsp (5 mL) sesame oil

pinch pepper

1½ tbsp (20 mL) cornstarch blended with 3 tbsp (45 mL) vegetable stock

12 large spring roll wrappers

1 egg white or 3 tbsp (45 mL) water

¼ lb (110 g) firm bean curd, sliced

5 tbsp (75 mL) plum sauce

1 Heat oil in a wok. Fry mushrooms, onions, garlic and ginger 1 minute. Add remaining vegetables and stir-fry 2 minutes. Blend in soy sauce, sesame oil and pepper.

2 Stir in combined cornstarch and vegetable stock to thicken pan juices. Place mixture in a large pan to cool. Divide filling into twelve portions. Arrange spring roll wrappers with one corner towards you. Brush edges with egg white. Place a portion of filling onto each skin, top with sliced bean curd. Fold lower point over filling. Fold left and right points into center. Brush with egg white again. Roll up firmly and stand on sealed edge.

3 Rolls can be deep-fried two or three at a time in vegetable oil until golden, or brushed with oil and oven-baked at 350°F (180°C) for 15 to 20 minutes. Serve with warm plum sauce.

SERVES 4–6

TOSSED RICE NOODLES WITH CHOP SUEY

¼ cup (60 mL) vegetable oil

1 tsp (5 mL) chopped fresh ginger

1 onion, shredded

¼ lb (110 g) broccoli florets

½ cup (125 mL) vegetable stock

½ lb (225 g) fresh mushrooms, cut in ½ inch (1 cm) slices

½ lb (225 g) bean sprouts, roots removed

5 oz (150 g) bamboo shoots, sliced

2 oz (60 g) water chestnuts, sliced

⅔ lb (300 g) bean curd cakes, diced

3 tbsp (45 mL) dry sherry

1 tsp (5 mL) sesame oil

1 lb (450 g) rice noodles, sliced

GARNISH

1 egg omelet, cut into thin strips

1 green onion, finely chopped

1 tbsp (15 mL) almond slivers, toasted

1 Heat oil in a wok. Add ginger, onion and broccoli, and stir-fry 1 minute. Add stock and cook covered 2 minutes. Add mushrooms, bean sprouts, bamboo shoots, water chestnuts, bean curd, sherry and sesame oil. Fold in noodles. Cover and simmer 1–2 minutes to heat through. Serve hot.

2 Garnish with shredded egg, green onion and almond slivers.

SERVES 4–6

Tossed Rice Noodles with Chop Suey

LOW FAT
AND LOW CHOLESTEROL DELIGHTS

The Chinese diet is traditionally low in fat and Chinese fare can be readily adapted for low cholesterol cooking. In part this is because meals are based on rice with delicious sauces made from vegetables, fruits and spices and a garnish of animal protein in the form of meat, fish or chicken.

By making your own sauces at home using fresh, natural ingredients, removing all visible fat from meat, chicken or duck and by quickly stir-frying in a non-stick pan or wok using a little stock or water, you can continue to enjoy many of your favorite recipes – including spring rolls. Usually deep-fried, spring rolls can be baked in the oven to produce a tasty appetizer for a low cholesterol meal.

Beef Fillet with Sweet and Sour Sauce and Steamed Dim Sum (page 70)

STEAMED DIM SUM

¼ lb (110 g) eggless wonton wrappers

2–3 tbsp (30–45 mL) peas

lettuce leaves, to steam

FILLING

½ lb (225 g) chicken, steamed and finely chopped

½ lb (225 g) firm white fish fillets, finely chopped

1 green onion, finely cut

⅓ cup (85 mL) chopped water chestnuts

4 Chinese mushrooms, soaked in warm water 20 minutes and finely chopped

1 tbsp (15 mL) salt-reduced soy sauce

pinch pepper

DIP SAUCE

3 tbsp (45 mL) salt-reduced soy sauce

1 tbsp (15 mL) white vinegar

1 Mix all filling ingredients together. Place 2–3 tsp (10–15 mL) filling in the center of each skin. Gather edges around filling in cup shape and press so that filling comes up to the edge of each skin. Place a pea on top of filling. The dim sum should have a flat base and stand upright.

2 Place a few lettuce leaves into a bamboo steamer. Arrange dim sum on top with enough space between them so they don't touch. Steam covered 20 minutes. Serve with sauce.

3 TO MAKE DIP SAUCE: Combine ingredients in a small bowl.

SERVES 4–6

BEEF FILLET WITH SWEET AND SOUR SAUCE

1 lb (450 g) beef fillet, cut in ½ inch (1 cm) cubes

1 tbsp (15 mL) salt-reduced soy sauce

¼ tsp (1 mL) five-spice powder

SWEET AND SOUR SAUCE

1 cup (250 mL) unsweetened pineapple juice

1 tbsp (15 mL) sugar

1 tbsp (15 mL) white vinegar

1 tbsp (15 mL) cornstarch

1 tbsp (15 mL) dry sherry

1 cup (250 mL) beef consommé

½ green pepper, cut in ½ inch (1 cm) dice

¼ carrot, parboiled, cut in ½ inch (1 cm) dice

¼ cup (60 mL) unsweetened pineapple pieces

¼ lb (110 g) diced Chinese mixed pickles

1 Combine diced beef with soy sauce and five-spice powder and marinate 15 minutes. Heat a non-stick pan, add one-quarter of the beef and stir-fry 3–4 minutes. Remove from pan. Repeat with remaining beef. Set aside and keep warm.

2 Bring pineapple juice, sugar and vinegar to a boil. Blend cornstarch, sherry and stock to a paste. Stir into pineapple juice to

thicken. Add vegetables, pineapple and pickles, simmer 3 minutes. Add diced beef to heat through. Serve at once.

SERVES 4–6

PUMPKIN AND FISH BALLS WITH BLACK BEAN SAUCE

1–1½ lbs (450-675 g) firm pumpkin or squash

¾ lb (340 g) fish balls (see page 36)

1 cup (250 mL) vegetable stock

SAUCE

1 tbsp (15 mL) fermented black beans, chopped

1 level tsp (5 mL) chopped garlic

1 tsp (5 mL) chopped fresh ginger

2 tbsp (30 mL) salt-reduced soy sauce

3 tbsp (45 mL) dry sherry

½ tsp (2.5 mL) sugar

pinch pepper

1½ tbsp (20 mL) cornstarch blended with 5 tbsp (75 mL) vegetable stock

1 Remove seeds from pumpkin. Using a melon baller, prepare even-sized pumpkin balls. Heat stock, add pumpkin balls and cook until just tender. Drain, retaining stock.

2 Reheat stock in a non-stick pan, add beans, garlic, ginger, soy sauce, sherry, sugar and pepper. Simmer 2 minutes. Add fish balls. Simmer covered 4–5 minutes. Add pumpkin balls to reheat. Stir in blended cornstarch and vegetable stock to thicken. Serve at once.

SERVES 4–6

❖ **NOTE**

Fish balls can be bought ready-made in Asian food stores or can be made at home.

Pumpkin and Fish Balls with Black Bean Sauce

BEEF WITH HOT BEAN SAUCE

½ lb (225 g) beef fillet, thinly sliced

1 tbsp (15 mL) dry sherry

¼ cup (60 mL) beef consommé

1 tsp (5 mL) chopped garlic

1 tbsp (15 mL) hot bean sauce

1 large onion, cut into eighths

2 tsp (10 mL) cornstarch

1 tsp (5 mL) salt-reduced soy sauce

¼ cup (60 mL) vegetable stock or water

1 Combine sliced beef and sherry. Heat a non-stick pan, add beef and stir-fry 2 minutes. Remove from pan and set aside.
2 Reheat pan, add consommé, garlic, hot bean sauce and onion, and simmer covered 2 minutes.
3 Return beef to pan. Blend cornstarch with soy sauce and stock. Stir in to thicken and serve at once.

SERVES 4

❖ **HINT**

Soak bamboo satay skewers in water to prevent burning.

CHICKEN AND VEGETABLE SATAY

½ lb (225 g) chicken breast, skin removed, cut in ¾ inch (2 cm) cubes

1 tbsp (15 mL) salt-reduced soy sauce

1 medium onion, quartered

¼ red pepper, cut into ¾ inch (2 cm) cubes

8 button mushrooms

4 long bamboo satay sticks, soaked in water to prevent burning

¼ cup (60 mL) orange juice

1 Combine chicken with soy sauce and let marinate 15 minutes. Thread chicken, onion, red pepper and mushrooms onto satay sticks. Place on a sheet of foil and brush with orange juice.
2 Broil under medium heat until chicken is white. Baste with orange juice frequently to prevent drying out. Serve with brown rice.

SERVES 4

FISH COCKTAILS WITH HONEY ORANGE SAUCE

1 lb (450 g) firm white fish fillets, cut in 1¼ inch (3 cm) cubes

3 tbsp (45 mL) salt-reduced soy sauce

3 tbsp (45 mL) honey

¼ cup (60 mL) fresh orange juice, strained

1 slice fresh ginger, shredded

cornstarch (optional)

1 Combine fish pieces, soy sauce, honey and orange juice. Marinate 15 minutes.
2 Place fish and marinade in a shallow heatproof dish. Sprinkle with ginger. Cover with a lid or foil. Steam over boiling water 12 minutes.
3 Drain off liquid and reheat it in a saucepan. Reduce by half or thicken with cornstarch. Serve over fish pieces.

SERVES 4

BEEF AND BROCCOLI

½ lb (225 g) beef fillet, thinly sliced

2 tsp (10 mL) salt-reduced soy sauce

⅓ cup (85 mL) vegetable stock

1 lb (450 g) broccoli florets

½ tsp (2.5 mL) sugar

½ tsp (2.5 mL) chopped fresh ginger

1 tbsp (15 mL) cornstarch blended with 3 tbsp (45 mL) vegetable stock

1 Combine sliced beef with soy sauce, and let marinate 15 minutes. Heat a non-stick pan. Add beef and stir-fry 1 minute. Remove from pan and set aside.
2 Add stock to pan and bring to a boil. Add broccoli, sugar and ginger, and cook covered over high heat 3 minutes.
3 Return beef to pan. Stir in blended cornstarch and stock to thicken. Serve at once.

SERVES 4–6

Beef with Hot Bean Sauce and Chicken and Vegetable Satay

Spaghetti Squash with Peking Sauce

1 Combine scallops with hoisin sauce. Thread onto skewers with diced onion. Place on sheet of foil and brush with a mixture of orange juice and soy sauce.

2 Broil under medium heat 2–4 minutes, until scallops are white. Brush with orange juice and soy sauce during cooking. The remaining juice can be thickened and served as a sauce.

SERVES 4

SWEET AND SOUR CABBAGE

¼ cup (60 mL) unsweetened pineapple juice

1 tsp (5 mL) chopped fresh ginger

1 medium onion, cut into eighths

2 red peppers, shredded

1 lb (450 g) cabbage, shredded

3 tbsp (45 mL) sugar or substitute

3 tbsp (45 mL) white vinegar

1 tbsp (15 mL) salt-reduced soy sauce

1 tbsp (15 mL) cornstarch

¼ cup (60 mL) stock

❖ **HINT**

Blend a large quantity of cornstarch with water in a jar. Store in refrigerator and shake jar to mix before using.

1 Heat pineapple juice in a non-stick pan. Add ginger, onion and red peppers, and stir-fry 2 minutes. Add cabbage and cook covered 2 minutes. Stir in sugar, vinegar and soy sauce.

2 Blend cornstarch with stock. Stir in to thicken. Serve at once.

SERVES 4

SCALLOP SATAY

1 lb (450 g) fresh scallops or thick white fish fillets

3 tbsp (45 mL) hoisin sauce

1 large onion, cut in ¾ inch (2 cm) cubes

8 small satay sticks, soaked in cold water

½ cup (125 mL) orange juice

1 tbsp (15 mL) salt-reduced soy sauce

SPAGHETTI SQUASH WITH PEKING SAUCE

1–1½ lbs (450–675 g) spaghetti squash in one piece

1½ cups (375 mL) vegetable stock

SAUCE

½ lb (225 g) lean ground veal

2 tsp (10 mL) dry sherry

½ cup (125 mL) onion, finely chopped

1 tbsp (15 mL) yellow bean sauce

3 tbsp (45 mL) salt-reduced soy sauce

1 tbsp (15 mL) hoisin sauce

1½ cups (375 mL) seasoned vegetable stock

1 tbsp (15 mL) finely chopped fresh coriander

1 **TO PREPARE SQUASH:** Leave skin on and remove seeds with a spoon. Place stock in a saucepan. Stand squash cut side up in saucepan, cover, and bring liquid to a boil. Simmer 20 minutes until squash is tender.

2 Remove squash and scrape out flesh in long strands from skin. Place on a warm serving platter.

3 **TO MAKE SAUCE:** Combine veal with sherry and onion in a non-stick pan. Stir-fry until veal loses its pink color. Add bean paste, soy and hoisin sauces with stock and simmer 20 minutes.

4 The sauce can be thickened slightly with cornstarch paste if desired. Serve poured over spaghetti squash and garnish with fresh coriander.

SERVES 4

HOT SOUR BEAN CURD SOUP

6 cups (1.5 L) vegetable stock

1 tbsp (15 mL) cornstarch

1 tsp (5 mL) grated fresh ginger

1 tbsp (15 mL) dry sherry

1 tbsp (15 mL) salt-reduced soy sauce

1 tbsp (15 mL) white vinegar

pinch cayenne pepper

½ lb (225 g) firm bean curd, cut into ½ inch (1 cm) cubes

1 egg white, lightly beaten

lettuce leaves, shredded

1 Blend stock with cornstarch and bring to a boil. Add ginger, sherry, soy sauce, vinegar and pepper. Simmer 2 minutes.
2 Add bean curd to heat through for 2 minutes. Pour in egg white. When set, add lettuce, serve at once.

SERVES 4–6

VEAL SPRING ROLLS

½ lb (225 g) lean veal steak, finely chopped

2 tsp (10 mL) salt-reduced soy sauce

1 tsp (5 mL) sugar

3 tbsp (45 mL) vegetable stock

4 Chinese mushrooms, soaked in warm water 20 minutes and shredded

½ lb (225 g) soybean sprouts, roots removed

1 onion, finely chopped

½ lb (225 g) cabbage, finely shredded

1½ tbsp (20 mL) cornstarch blended with 3 tbsp (45 mL) vegetable stock

12 large eggless spring roll wrappers

DIP

5 tbsp (75 mL) plum sauce combined with few drops chili pepper sauce

1 Combine veal, soy sauce and sugar and let stand 15 minutes. Heat vegetable stock in a non-stick frying pan. Add veal and stir-fry lightly. Add mushrooms, bean sprouts, onion and cabbage and stir-fry for a few minutes.

2 Stir in blended cornstarch and stock to thicken pan juices. Remove mixture. Allow to cool.
3 Divide mixture into 12 portions. Arrange spring roll wrappers with a corner pointing towards you. Place a portion of filling in center. Fold bottom point over filling. Fold sides to center. Brush with cold water. Roll up firmly. Place on an ungreased pan and bake at 400°F (200°C) 20–30 minutes. Serve with dip sauce.

SERVES 6

BRAISED MIXED VEGETABLES

½ cup (125 mL) vegetable stock

1 tsp (5 mL) chopped fresh ginger

½ tsp (2.5 mL) chopped garlic

½ tsp (2.5 mL) sugar

¼ lb (110 g) broccoli florets

1 large onion, cut into eighths

¼ lb (110 g) Chinese long beans, cut into 1 inch (2.5 cm) lengths

4 oz (110 g) bamboo shoots, sliced

4 oz (110 g) straw mushrooms

1 tbsp (15 mL) salt-reduced soy sauce

1 tbsp (15 mL) oyster sauce

1 tbsp (15 mL) dry sherry

2 tsp (10 mL) cornstarch

1 Bring stock to a boil in a pan. Add ginger, garlic, sugar, broccoli, onion and beans. Cover, and cook on high heat 3–4 minutes. Add bamboo shoots and straw mushrooms.
2 Blend soy and oyster sauces with sherry and cornstarch. Stir into vegetable mixture to thicken slightly. Serve at once.

SERVES 4–6

❖ **HINT**

Braise long-cooking dishes in advance. Divide into serving portions and freeze.

ABOUT CHOLESTEROL

It is now clear that reducing the amount of fat in our diet has significant health benefits for us all. Fat, whether saturated or unsaturated, is a concentrated source of calories (kilojoules). In addition, high fat diets have been linked to the development of other diseases including gallbladder disease and some cancers. Recent research shows that reducing food fat, particularly saturated fat, has a more direct influence on blood cholesterol than does food cholesterol. For most people it is better to cut down on saturated fats than to eliminate nutritious foods such as eggs, shellfish and liver which are high in cholesterol. Below is a list of the main foods containing fat. Many foods contain a mixture of saturated, monounsaturated and polyunsaturated fats, so the foods are classified according to the predominant fat.

SATURATED FAT Butter, cream, drippings, lard; coconut oil, palm oil; many cheeses, ice cream, chocolate; meat fat, poultry skin; full cream dairy products; many commercial foods including snack foods, pies, pastries, biscuits, fast foods, chips and French fries.

MONOUNSATURATED FAT Olive oil, olives; peanut oil, peanuts, peanut butter; most nuts; avocado; egg yolk; margarine (unless labelled polyunsaturated); lean meat, chicken, salmon, tuna.

POLYUNSATURATED FAT Most vegetable oils, including safflower, sunflower, canola, corn, cotton seed, soybean, grape seed, walnut, sesame; margarine, reduced-fat spreads and oils labelled polyunsaturated; seeds, including sunflower, pumpkin, sesame; nuts: walnuts, brazil nuts, pine nuts; fish, shellfish.

LOW CHOLESTEROL COOKING MADE EASY

REDUCE FATS Reduce your intake of all fats. Only 30 percent of your total calorie intake should come from fats, with saturated fats contributing no more that 10 percent and unsaturated fats (poly- and monounsaturated) contributing the remaining 20 percent.

REDUCE CHOLESTEROL Reduce your cholesterol intake from foods to under 300 milligrams a day. Limit cholesterol-rich foods such as brains, liver, kidney, egg yolks, shrimp, fish roe and squid.

REDUCE SALT Reduce your salt intake. Do not sprinkle salt on food or in cooking, and switch to salt-reduced or no-added-salt products.

INCREASE FIBER Increase your fiber intake. Oats, oat bran, barley, barley bran, rice, rice bran, dried beans, lentils, fruit and vegetables.

COLD SUMMER NOODLES

1 lb (450 g) eggless curry-flavored noodles

6 cups (1.5 L) vegetable stock

½ lb (225 g) chicken breast, steamed and shredded

½ lb (225 g) fresh bean sprouts, roots removed and blanched

1 English (seedless) cucumber, cut in half lengthwise and shredded

1 tsp (5 mL) chopped garlic

¼ cup (60 mL) vinegar

¼ cup (60 mL) salt-reduced soy sauce

1 Cook noodles in boiling stock 4 minutes. Drain and cool, discarding stock.

2 Combine chicken, bean sprouts and cucumber. Add garlic, vinegar and soy sauce. Add to noodles, toss to blend. Serve chilled.

SERVES 4

EGGPLANT WITH BEAN CURD AND BASIL

1 tbsp (15 mL) vegetable oil

1 tsp (5 mL) chopped garlic

½ lb (225 g) firm bean curd, cut in ¾ inch (2 cm) cubes

1 medium eggplant, peeled and cut in ¾ inch (2 cm) cubes

4 ripe tomatoes, peeled and quartered

½ tsp (2.5 mL) sugar

¼ tsp (1 mL) dried basil

½ tsp (2.5 mL) salt

¼ tsp (1 mL) pepper

½ cup (125 mL) vegetable stock

1 Heat oil in a wok. Lightly fry garlic and bean curd. Add eggplant, tomatoes, sugar, basil, salt, pepper and stock. Bring to a boil, then simmer gently until eggplant is tender. The mixture may be thickened slightly with cornstarch if preferred.

SERVES 6

STIR-FRIED CHICKEN WITH BEAN SPROUTS

¼ cup (60 mL) vegetable stock

¼ lb (110 g) fresh chicken breast, skinned and shredded

1 lb (450 g) bean sprouts, roots removed

2 tsp (10 mL) cornstarch

2 tsp (10 mL) dry sherry

¼ tsp (1 mL) sugar

1 tbsp (15 mL) salt-reduced soy sauce

1 Heat stock in a non-stick pan. Add chicken strips and stir-fry 3 minutes. Add bean sprouts. Cook covered 2 minutes. Blend cornstarch, sherry, sugar and soy sauce. Stir in to thicken. Serve at once.

2 Serve garnished with green onion shreds.

SERVES 4

CHICKEN AND VEGETABLE SOUP

½ lb (225 g) chicken breast, bones and skin removed

2 Chinese mushrooms, soaked in warm water 20 minutes and sliced

2 tsp (10 mL) dry sherry

6 cups (1.5 L) vegetable stock

⅓ stalk celery, sliced

½ carrot, cut in thin strips

1 tsp (5 mL) cornstarch blended with 2 tsp (10 mL) stock or water

1 tbsp (15 mL) finely chopped fresh coriander or green onions

1 Cut chicken meat into thin strips. Cover with boiling water. Let stand 2 minutes. Drain, then repeat process – this ensures the chicken is free of any hidden fat. Sprinkle mushrooms with sherry and let stand.

2 Bring stock to a boil, add chicken, mushrooms, celery and carrots. Simmer covered 5 minutes. Blend cornstarch with stock, stir in to thicken soup. When boiling, sprinkle soup with coriander and serve.

SERVES 4–6

❖ **HINT**

Freeze fresh noodles, wonton wrappers and spring roll wrappers in recipe size amounts.

RICE
AND NOODLES

Rice and noodles are staple fare in the Chinese diet. Rice is
grown and eaten primarily in the southern part of China; other grains
including wheat, millet and sorghum predominate in the north.
But to the Chinese, the flavor of rice is the perfect accompaniment
to all other foods. When sampling all the myriad taste elements
of a Chinese meal, a spoonful of rice taken with the other food
as well as in between brings a neutral element into play so that every
new morsel can unfold all its full flavor and character.

Long-grain rice is suitable for most dishes. When properly
cooked, rice absorbs a great deal of water and will be dry and fluffy.
Rice is either boiled or steamed. It is very important to wash the rice well
to remove the excess starch which otherwise will make the rice too sticky.
After it has been boiled or steamed, cooked rice can be fried,
but it should be completely cooled first.

Noodles are the food of the north. They are made mainly from grains,
but sometimes from seaweed or the starch of mung beans.
Noodles can be boiled, steamed, soft-fried, deep-fried and used in soups.

Fresh Egg Noodle Baskets and Three Jeweled
Chicken In Noodle Baskets (page 80)

POTATO NESTS OR BASKETS

1 lb (450 g) grated potato

3 tbsp (45 mL) cornstarch

salt and pepper

oil, for frying

1 Combine potato, cornstarch and seasonings. Dip basket molds or wire strainers into hot oil. Place 4–5 tbsp (60–75 mL) potato mixture into the larger basket. Arrange to cover surface of basket. Place smaller basket on top. Holding the handles of both baskets together, dip into hot oil to cover.

2 When the potato sets, the smaller mold can be removed. Continue cooking until crisp and golden.

3 Use for serving deep- or stir-fried food.

MAKES 4–6 BASKETS

❖ **ROAST DUCK**

Roast duck should be available from specialty Chinese shops, or you may prepare you own. Marinate duck pieces in char sui marinade and cook as for char sui.

CONGEE ROAST DUCK

¾ cup (185 mL) uncooked rice

6 cups (1.5 L) water

2 small dried scallops, 3 tbsp (45 mL) dried shrimp or 1½ tsp (7.5 mL) salt

1 small piece dried tangerine or orange peel

½ roast duck, cut into bite-size pieces

1 tbsp (15 mL) sherry

3 tbsp (45 mL) sliced green onions

1 Place rice and water in a pan. Add scallops and tangerine peel. Bring to a boil over high heat. Reduce heat, cover and simmer for 45 minutes.

2 Add roast duck and sherry to rice. Cover and simmer for at least 1 hour, stirring occasionally and adding some water if the congee becomes too thick. Remove tangerine peel and dried scallops, if desired. Top with green onions and serve.

SERVES 4

THREE JEWELED CHICKEN IN NOODLE BASKETS

vermicelli noodle baskets (see below)

FILLING

½ lb (225 g) boneless chicken breast, thinly sliced

1 tsp (5 mL) cornstarch

2 tsp (10 mL) egg white

3 tbsp (45 mL) vegetable oil

2 tbsp (30 mL) ginger in syrup, sliced

4 oz (110 g) canned lychees

4 oz (110 g) canned loquats

SAUCE

1 tbsp (15 mL) cornstarch

3 tbsp (45 mL) light soy sauce

3 tbsp (45 mL) white vinegar

3 tbsp (45 mL) sugar

½ cup (125 mL) lychee juice

1 Combine chicken, cornstarch and egg white in a bowl. Heat oil in a wok. Stir-fry chicken until white. Add ginger, lychees and loquats.

2 Combine sauce ingredients. Stir into chicken and heat until thickened.

3 Serve mixture in noodle baskets.

MAKES 6 INDIVIDUAL BASKETS OR 2 LARGE BASKETS

❖ **VARIATIONS**

Fresh egg noodle baskets: Divide 2 oz (60 g) fresh egg noodles into 6 portions, and line 6 basket molds. Cook as for Potato Nests.

Vermicelli nests or baskets: Cut 1 oz (28 g) vermicelli noodles into 1 inch (2.5 cm) lengths. Line a large mold and cook as for Potato Nests.

STEP-BY-STEP TECHNIQUES

CRISPY NOODLES

¾ lb (340 g) egg noodles (preferably fresh)

3 tbsp (45 mL) oil

1 onion, shredded

½ bunch celery, shredded

½ lb (225 g) chicken or pork, shredded

1 tbsp (15 mL) soy sauce

oil, for deep-frying

1 Cook noodles. Drain, rinse well and set aside. After about 10 minutes, turn out noodles onto a tray and separate them with chopsticks or a fork.

2 Heat oil in a wok and stir-fry vegetables and meat together for about 5–6 minutes. While still crisp, season with soy sauce and keep warm.

3 Put ¼ of the noodles into a strainer, heat the oil for deep-frying and plunge strainer into the oil; fry until noodles are crisp then drain on paper towels. Turn onto serving dish and top with meat and vegetable sauce.

SERVES 4

1 *Cook noodles, drain and rinse well. After 10 minutes, turn onto a tray and separate with chopsticks.*

2 *Heat oil in a wok and stir-fry meat and vegetables together for 5–6 minutes.*

3 *Put noodles in a strainer, heat oil for deep-frying and plunge strainer into the oil. Fry until crisp then drain on paper towels.*

FRIED RICE WITH BEEF AND ALMONDS

½ lb (225 g) lean steak, thinly sliced and shredded

1 tbsp (15 mL) soy sauce

1 tbsp (15 mL) cornstarch

3 tbsp (45 mL) vegetable oil

1 large onion, cut in fine shreds

1 medium green pepper, cut in fine shreds

½ tsp (2.5 mL) salt

2 cups (500 mL) hot steamed rice

4 oz (110 g) almonds, toasted

GARNISH

green onion shreds

extra toasted almonds

1 Combine steak, soy sauce and cornstarch. Heat oil in a wok and add steak mixture. Stir-fry 2 minutes. Add onion, green pepper and salt. Stir-fry 1 minute. Add rice and almonds, stir-frying to blend ingredients. This can be done off the heat.

2 Place mixture into an oiled ring mold. Press down firmly. Turn out onto round serving plate, garnish and serve.

SERVES 6

❖ **HINT**

Deep-fry chow mein noodles, drain well and store in an air-tight container.

PORK FRIED RICE

1½ cups (375 mL) uncooked rice

4 tbsp (60 mL) oil

2 eggs, lightly beaten

1 clove garlic, bruised

1 slice fresh ginger, roughly chopped

6 green onions, cut in ½ inch (1 cm) pieces

½ lb (225 g) Chinese barbecued pork (char sui)

¼ cup (60 mL) soy sauce

1 Cook rice. Heat 1 tbsp (15 mL) oil in a wok. Pour in beaten eggs to form a flat omelet; cook for 2 minutes. When bottom is set, flip over and cook for further 2 minutes. Remove from heat, roll up jelly-roll style and cut into thin strips.

2 Heat remaining oil in wok, add garlic and ginger and cook until browned, lift out and discard. Add green onions and rice. Stir-fry 2–3 minutes. Add char sui and soy sauce, and stir-fry 1 minute. Add a little water if too dry. Spoon rice into a serving dish and garnish with egg strips.

SERVES 4

COMBINATION SEAFOOD CHOW MEIN

½ lb (225 g) crisp-fried fresh egg noodles (see page 85)

¼ lb (110 g) shrimp meat, deveined

¼ lb (110 g) scallops

¼ lb (110 g) prepared squid

¼ lb (110 g) sliced fish fillets

½ tsp (2.5 mL) chopped fresh ginger

3 tbsp (45 mL) cornstarch

3 tbsp (45 mL) light soy sauce

3 tbsp (45 mL) sherry

5 tbsp (75 mL) oil

½ tsp (2.5 mL) salt

4 stalks Chinese cabbage, cut in 1 inch (2.5 cm) pieces

1 cup (250 mL) sliced bamboo shoots

6 oz (180 g) straw mushrooms, sliced lengthwise

1 Arrange crisp-fried fresh egg noodles on serving platter and keep warm.

2 Combine seafood, ginger, cornstarch, soy sauce and sherry, toss to coat.

3 Heat 3 tbsp (45 mL) oil. Add seafood and stir-fry 2–3 minutes. Remove from pan.

4 Heat remaining oil. Add salt and Chinese cabbage stalks, and stir-fry 1 minute.

5 Add cabbage leaves, bamboo shoots and mushrooms. Cover and cook 2 minutes.

6 Return seafood to reheat. Serve over crisp noodles.

SERVES 6–8

Pork Fried Rice

BARBECUED PORK CHOW MEIN

3 tbsp (45 mL) vegetable oil

1 tsp (5 mL) chopped fresh ginger

1 tsp (5 mL) chopped garlic

½ lb (225 g) Chinese barbecued pork (char sui)

4 Chinese mushrooms, soaked in warm water 20 minutes and sliced

2 oz (60 g) carrot, sliced and parboiled

½ lb (225 g) broccoli florets, blanched

2 oz (60 g) bamboo shoots, sliced

¼ lb (110 g) bean sprouts, roots removed

½ cup (125 mL) stock

3 tbsp (45 mL) light soy sauce

1 tbsp (15 mL) dry sherry

1 tsp (5 mL) sugar

1½ tbsp (20 mL) cornstarch blended with 3 tbsp (45 mL) water

½ lb (225 g) soft-fried noodles (see page 85)

1 Heat oil in a wok. Add ginger, garlic, pork and stir-fry 1-2 minutes. Add vegetables, stock, soy sauce, sherry and sugar. Simmer covered for 2 minutes.

2 Stir in combined cornstarch and water to thicken. Serve over hot noodles.

SERVES 6

❖ FRIED RICE

When cooking rice for fried rice, steam in advance. Spread onto a tray and refrigerate until required. Cooked rice will freeze and defrost well.

RICE

Rice is one of the best sources of nutrition and nourishment around the world. Brown rice is better nutritional value than white rice, but both can be useful in our diets, as they are:

❖ high in protein and dietary fibre
❖ high in vitamins and minerals – calcium, iron, thiamine, riboflavin and niacin
❖ low in fat, salt and sugar
❖ cholesterol-free

On the question of how much to use, the general rule is ½ cup (125 mL) uncooked rice per person. If steaming, allow 2 cups (500 mL) water for the first cup of rice, and 1½ cups (375 mL) water for each additional cup of rice.

❖ **STEAMED RICE**

Rinse rice with cold water several times. Place rice in a medium-size saucepan and cover with cold water to ¾ inch (2 cm) above the rice. Bring to a boil. Stir once and cook uncovered until air bubble holes form. Reduce heat to low. Cover and steam for 20 minutes. Remove from heat and allow to stand covered 5 minutes. Stir rice grains with a fork to loosen, avoiding cutting through grains. Steamed rice will remain hot in the saucepan for over 30 minutes. During this time several stir-fry dishes can be prepared.

CHINESE RICE

2½ cups (625 mL) uncooked rice

water

1 Wash rice in cold water until water runs clear. Place rice in saucepan and cover with water to 1 inch (2.5 cm) above rice level. Bring to a boil, reduce heat to medium and continue cooking, uncovered, until water evaporates (air bubble holes will form through rice.)

2 When water has evaporated, place lid on saucepan and continue cooking for 7 minutes on low heat. Do not stir or lift lid during last 7 minutes of cooking. If not using immediately, leave in covered pan.

SERVES 4–6

FRIED RICE

2 cups (500 mL) cold cooked rice

3 eggs, beaten lightly

1 tbsp (15 mL) light soy sauce

¼ tsp (1 mL) sesame oil

salt and pepper

3 tbsp (45 mL) vegetable oil

¼ lb (110 g) cooked shrimp meat, cut in ¼ inch (0.5 cm) dice (optional)

2 slices cooked bacon, drained, cut in ¼ inch (0.5 cm) dice or ¼ lb (110 g) char sui

2 green onions, chopped

1 Use chopsticks or a fork to separate the rice grains.

2 In a small bowl, combine the eggs, soy sauce, sesame oil and salt and pepper. Set aside.

3 Heat wok. Add oil by pouring it around the rim. This seals the wok and heats the oil quickly. Add shrimp, if using, bacon and green onion. Immediately add rice and stir-fry over high heat; after a few minutes the grains will separate.

4 While stirring rice, pour in egg mixture. Stir-fry 1 minute. Serve rice in a warm Chinese bowl to retain heat during serving.

SERVES 6

Fried Rice: Use chopsticks to separate cooked grains of rice.

Add rice grains to stir-fried bacon and onions.

Pour in egg mixture while stirring.

NOODLES

In China, noodles are traditionally the food of the north. They are made mainly from grains, but sometimes also from seaweed or the starch of mung beans. Noodles are almost always made in thin threads, but there is considerable variety in texture, thickness and width. They can be boiled, steamed, soft-fried, deep-fried and used in soups. These days, they are often available from larger supermarkets and delicatessens, as well as from Oriental food stores and Chinese grocers.

DRIED NOODLES

Dried long-life egg and eggless noodles are available in various styles. The noodles can be thin, round or flat and come in 2 oz (60 g) bundles, usually 6-8 bundles per package. Dried noodles are also available flavored e.g. chicken, shrimp, beef and curry.

CHINESE NOODLES

4-5 cups (1 – 1.25 L) water
1 tsp (5 mL) salt
8 oz (225 g) dried noodles
vegetable or sesame oil
TO SOFT-FRY NOODLES
5 tbsp (75 mL) vegetable oil
½ tsp (2.5 mL) salt

1 Bring water to a boil. Add salt, then noodles. Stir with chopsticks to loosen each bundle. Cooking should be completed in 3–5 minutes. Do not overcook; remember noodles will also be fried. Drain well, rinse in cold water. Drain and spread loosely on a tray. Sprinkle with a little oil and refrigerate for 2 hours before frying.

2 Heat oil with salt. When very hot, carefully add cooked noodles. Use tongs or chopsticks to loosen noodles. Reduce heat and fry noodles for 2 minutes. Turn noodles over and cook another 2 minutes. The noodles should be lightly brown and crisp on the outside.

SERVES 4

Fried Noodles with Chicken and Vegetables

FRIED NOODLES WITH CHICKEN AND VEGETABLES

½ lb (225 g) fresh egg noodles
oil, for deep-frying
1 whole chicken breast, skinned and boned
½ lb (225 g) uncooked shrimp, peeled
1 clove garlic, crushed
1 piece bamboo shoot, shredded
6 Chinese mushrooms, soaked in warm water 20 minutes and sliced
¼ lb (110 g) vegetables (e.g. celery, green onions, beans), cut into matchsticks
½ cup (125 mL) stock
½ tsp (2.5 mL) cornstarch
1 tbsp (15 mL) soy sauce
pinch five-spice powder

1 Divide noodles into four portions. Deep-fry each portion in hot oil until golden brown. Drain on paper towels.

2 Cut chicken meat into strips. Heat wok, add 1 tbsp (15 mL) vegetable oil and stir-fry chicken and shrimp with garlic. Add bamboo shoot, mushrooms and vegetables and stir-fry for a further 5 minutes.

3 Pour in stock, cornstarch dissolved in soy sauce and five-spice powder and simmer for 5 minutes.

4 TO SERVE: Place noodles on a plate and spoon chicken and vegetables on top.

SERVES 4

❖ **CRISP-FRIED FRESH EGG NOODLES**

Heat 1½ cups (375 mL) oil in a wok. Test temperature with a strand of noodle. If it crisps up quickly, the oil is the correct temperature. Separate ½ lb (225 g) fresh egg noodles into two batches. Carefully lower into the oil, one batch at a time. Cook 2 minutes, turn over with tongs and continue cooking until crisp and golden.

SAUCES
AND DIPS

The Chinese have two main categories of sauces.
Some sauces are incorporated into the dish and
mixed with the other ingredients by the cook. The other group of sauces
are served at the table as dipping sauces.

Marinades are also widely used in Chinese cooking to flavor
and tenderize the food before it is actually cooked.

❖ PEPPER AND SALT MIX

*Heat a wok until very
hot. Add 4 tbsp (60 mL)
salt and 3 tbsp (45 mL)
Szechuan peppercorns or
crushed peppercorns.
Reduce the heat and stir
5–6 minutes or until salt
is light brown.
Crush mixture in a
mortar and pestle and
sift through a sieve. Store
in a tightly covered jar.*

SHERRY-SOY DIP

3 tbsp (45 mL) sherry

3 tbsp (45 mL) soy sauce

¼ tsp (1 mL) sugar

1 Combine all ingredients and stir
together until the sugar has dissolved.

MAKES ⅓ CUP (85 mL)

SWEET AND SOUR GINGER SAUCE

½ cup (125 mL) sugar

2½ inch (6 cm) slice fresh ginger, finely chopped

½ cup (125 mL) vinegar

½ cup (125 mL) pineapple juice

1 tbsp (15 mL) sherry

2 tbsp (30 mL) cornstarch blended with ⅓ cup (85 mL) water

4 oz (110 g) Chinese pickle, thinly sliced

1 In a saucepan, combine sugar, ginger,
vinegar, pineapple juice and sherry. Bring to
a boil and stir in blended cornstarch and
water to thicken. Stir in Chinese pickle.

MAKES ABOOUT 2 CUPS (500 mL)

PLUM SAUCE

10 fresh plums, pitted and finely chopped

¼ cup (60 mL) dried apricots, soaked in warm water 1 hour and finely chopped

1 tsp (5 mL) chili pepper sauce

1 tsp (5 mL) salt

3 tbsp (45 mL) water

½ cup (125 mL) sugar

½ cup (125 mL) vinegar

1 Place plums and apricots in a wok. Add
chili pepper sauce, salt and water. Bring
to a boil and simmer gently 15 minutes.
Add a little more water if the mixture
becomes too dry.

2 Stir in sugar and vinegar and simmer
20–30 minutes until the sauce reaches a
chutney-like consistency. Pour sauce into a
sterilized jar, cover and refrigerate when
cool. This sauce will keep several months.

MAKES ABOUT 1 CUP (250 mL)

SWEET AND SOUR FRUITY SAUCE

½ cup (125 mL) sugar

½ cup (125 mL) vinegar

3 tbsp (45 mL) soy sauce

3 tbsp (45 mL) sherry

¼ cup (60 mL) tomato catsup

3 tbsp (45 mL) cornstarch blended with ½ cup (125 mL) pineapple juice

1 In a saucepan, combine sugar, vinegar, soy sauce, sherry and catsup. Bring to a boil and add cornstarch and pineapple juice mixture, stirring constantly until the sauce is thickened.

MAKES ABOUT 1½ CUPS (375 ML)

SWEET AND SOUR SAUCE

½ cup (125 mL) sugar

½ cup (125 mL) vinegar

5–6 tbsp (75–90 mL) light soy sauce

1 tbsp (15 mL) dark soy sauce (optional)

3 tbsp (45 mL) sherry

2 tbsp (30 mL) cornstarch blended with ½ cup (125 mL) water

1 In a saucepan, combine sugar, vinegar, light soy sauce, dark soy sauce and sherry. Bring to a boil and stir in the blended cornstarch and water to thicken.

MAKES ABOUT 1½ CUPS (375 ML)

GINGER-SOY DIP

3 tbsp (45 mL) oil

1 tbsp (15 mL) finely chopped green onions, white part only

½ tsp (2.5 mL) finely grated fresh ginger

5 tbsp (75 mL) soy sauce

1 Heat oil in a wok. Add green onions and ginger and stir-fry 30 seconds. Add soy sauce and remove from heat.

MAKES ABOUT ⅔ CUP (165 ML)

DESSERTS

The Chinese very rarely eat desserts, reserving them for banquets, formal dinners, or one of the many festivals that the Chinese celebrate.

Fresh fruit in season is a good choice for people who like to finish a meal with something sweet. Fortune cookies are always baked commercially and are available, in packages, from Chinese specialty stores. Moon cakes, which are also available from stores, are never prepared at home as they are time-consuming and require a long list of unusual ingredients. The cakes are filled with a lightly sweetened, rich-red soybean paste and are exchanged as gifts at the Moon Festival, during September.

Fruit ices are another suitable dessert for a Chinese meal. Marco Polo was introduced to these on his voyage to China and brought the idea back to the Western world.

Mandarin Sherbet (page 90) and Lychee and Ginger Mousse (page 91)

Toffee Apples

TOFFEE APPLES

4 ripe apples

1 egg

1 egg white

3 tbsp (45 mL) all-purpose flour

3 tbsp (45 mL) cornstarch

oil for deep-frying

¼ cup (60 mL) vegetable oil

¼ cup (60 mL) sugar

¼ cup (60 mL) honey

2 tbsp (30 mL) white sesame seeds (optional)

1 bowl ice water

1 Peel and core apples and cut each apple in six to eight wedges. Beat egg and egg white together and fold in sifted flour and cornstarch to make a batter.

2 Heat oil for deep-frying. Dip apple wedges in batter and deep-fry until golden. Remove and drain on paper towels.

3 In a saucepan heat vegetable oil, add sugar and heat, stirring constantly, until sugar dissolves. Stir in honey.

4 Coat apple fritters with syrup and sprinkle with sesame seeds.

5 Serve while piping hot. Let each guest dip apple fritters into ice water. This will cause the syrup coating to harden so the fritters will be crisp and crackling on the outside.

NOTE: Toffee apples can be prepared in advance to the stage of dipping in the syrup.

SERVES 4

MANDARIN SHERBET

1 lb (450 g) mandarins

1¼ cups (310 mL) white sugar

1¾ cups (450 mL) water

2 egg whites

1 Peel mandarins. Using a teaspoon, scrape the underside of the skin to remove any white pith from the zest. Cut the zest into thin strips. Combine zest, sugar and water in a saucepan. Heat until sugar completely dissolves. Raise heat and boil syrup for 5 minutes. Remove from heat and cool completely.

2 Squeeze juice from mandarins and strain. Strain syrup and combine with mandarin juice. Freeze mixture until partially frozen, stirring occasionally.

3 Whisk egg whites until stiff. Beat into soft ice mixture. Freeze until ice is firmer. Whisk again until smooth. Return to freezer until firm. Serve using small ice cream scoop.

SERVES 4–6

LYCHEE AND GINGER MOUSSE

14 oz (400 g) can lychees, drained (juice reserved)

1 tbsp (15 mL) ginger in syrup, drained and chopped

1 tbsp (15 mL) syrup from the preserved ginger

2 tsp (10 mL) gelatine

1¼ cups (310 mL) whipping cream, whipped

3 egg whites, beaten

1 Chop most of the lychees with the ginger. Place gelatine in a heatproof bowl, add 3 tbsp (45 mL) reserved lychee juice and dissolve over hot water.

2 Lightly fold whipped cream into egg whites. Add lychee mixture, reserved ginger syrup and gelatine, stir gently until well combined.

3 Pour into six individual bowls and refrigerate until set. Top with remaining fruit and rosettes of cream.

4 Alternatively, the mixture can be set in a wetted ring mold and served whole, garnished with extra fruit and cream.

SERVES 4–6

ALMOND FLOAT

2½ cups (625 mL) milk

¼ cup (60 mL) sugar

almond extract

2 tbsp (30 mL) gelatine

½ cup (125 mL) water

selection of prepared fresh fruit and canned lychees

1 Scald milk, remove from heat and add sugar. Cool slightly then add almond extract; cool. Sprinkle gelatine over water and leave until water is absorbed. Dissolve gelatine over hot water and cool. Stir into milk mixture.

2 When ready to serve, cut almond gelatine into diamond shapes. Place fruit in a serving bowl and arrange diamond shapes on top.

SERVES 4

RAMBUTAN COCKTAIL

20 oz (565 g) can rambutan fruit, drained

1 lb (450 g) honeydew melon balls

1 lb (450 g) cantaloupe balls

1 tbsp (15 mL) orange liqueur

1 egg white

¼ cup (60 mL) white sugar mixed with a few drops green food coloring

chilled sparkling white wine

1 Combine fruit and liqueur.

2 Place egg white and sugar on two separate plates. Invert six dessert glasses and dip rim into egg white, then into colored sugar. Fill glasses with assorted fruit and liqueur. Cover with sparkling wine. Serve chilled.

NOTE: Rambutan is a bright red fruit, oval in shape, which comes from Malaysia. It is available fresh or canned at supermarkets. If you need to substitute, you can use lychees or mangosteen.

SERVES 4–6

❖ **FRUITS**

Many oriental fruits are available canned and may be served individually with ice cream or combined for a fruit salad.

The most popular are lychees, longans, rambutan, mangosteen, mandarin quarters and jackfruit.

Almond Float

SNOW BALLS

2 cups (500 mL) glutinous rice flour

¼ cup (60 mL) cornstarch

3 tbsp (45 mL) white sugar

1 tbsp (15 mL) shortening

¾ cup (185 mL) water

3 oz (90 g) red bean paste

¼ cup (60 mL) cashew nuts, chopped

2 cups (500 mL) shredded coconut

½ lb (225 g) cherries or strawberries, to garnish

1 Combine rice and cornstarch with sugar. Work in shortening, add water and stir with a knife to form a dough. Knead 2–3 minutes. Roll dough into a sausage shape and divide into 16 pieces. Shape into balls.

2 Combine bean paste and cashew nuts. Divide into 16 portions. Make an indentation or hollow in each dough ball. Fill each with paste mixture, draw edges together to enclose filling. Reshape into a ball.

3 Cook in boiling water 8 minutes, stirring gently to prevent sticking on bottom of saucepan. Remove balls with a strainer. Cool slightly, then roll in coconut. Decorate each with half a cherry or strawberry. Store at room temperature.

VARIATION: 1 cup (250 mL) of coconut can be lightly toasted. Roll half the balls in white and half in toasted coconut.

SERVES 4–6

FRESH FRUIT ROLLS

1 firm ripe mango, peeled and cut in ¾ inch (2 cm) cubes

3 slices ripe fresh pineapple, peeled and cut in ¾ inch (2 cm) cubes

1 large apple, peeled and cut in ¾ inch (2 cm) cubes

3 kiwi fruit, peeled and cut in ¾ inch (2 cm) cubes

3 firm bananas, peeled and cut in ¾ inch (2 cm) cubes

½ lb (225 g) strawberries

1 tbsp (15 mL) orange liqueur

6–8 large spring roll wrappers

1 egg white, beaten

vegetable oil, for frying

icing sugar

vanilla ice cream

1 Combine fruit in a bowl. Sprinkle with liqueur and stand 15 minutes; drain. Divide fruit between spring roll wrappers. Brush edges with egg white. Roll up as for ordinary spring rolls.

2 Fry three rolls at a time in oil to cover. When golden, remove and drain well.

3 Dust with icing sugar and serve with ice cream.

SERVES 6–8

FRIED FRUIT BON BONS

4 oz (110 g) dried apricots, finely chopped

4 oz (110 g) dates, finely chopped

2 oz (60 g) crystallized ginger, finely chopped

¾ cup (185 mL) pecans or cashews, chopped

1½ tsp (7 mL) chopped orange zest

1 tbsp (15 mL) orange liqueur or orange juice

8 oz (225 g) wonton wrappers

vegetable oil, for frying

icing sugar

1 Combine apricots, dates, ginger, pecans, orange zest and liqueur. Roll 1 tbsp (15 mL) of filling in hands to make cylinder 1 inch (2.5 cm) long.

2 Place filling across wonton wrapper. Moisten edges with water. Roll up to seal, twisting ends.

3 Fry bon bons in oil to cover until crisp. Drain well. Dust with icing sugar and serve with Chinese tea.

SERVES 4–6

ASSORTED FRUIT FRITTERS

1 large firm mango, peeled

4 firm bananas, peeled

4 slices fresh pineapple

all-purpose flour, for dusting

¼ tsp (1 mL) cinnamon

BATTER

2 cups (500 mL) all-purpose flour

1 tsp (5 mL) baking powder

¼ tsp (1 mL) salt

⅔ cup (165 mL) milk

⅔ cup (165 mL) cold water

vegetable oil, for deep-frying

icing sugar

1 Cut fruit into serving pieces. Combine flour and cinnamon and lightly dust fruit.

2 TO MAKE BATTER: Sift flour, baking powder and salt into a bowl. Combine milk and water, and beat into flour to form a smooth batter. Strain before using.

3 Dip fruit into batter and fry in hot oil to cover until golden. Drain well. Arrange on serving platter. Sprinkle with icing sugar.

SERVES 6–8

MONGOLIAN RICE PUDDING

5 tbsp (75 mL) brown rice

1 cup (250 mL) water

2½ cups (625 mL) milk or soy milk

½ cup (125 mL) sugar

½ cup (125 mL) walnuts, coarsely chopped

¼ cup (60 mL) raisins

cinnamon or nutmeg

1 Put rice and water in a saucepan. Cook until water has been absorbed. Add milk and sugar and cook over low heat until mixture thickens. Add walnuts and raisins.

2 Serve hot, sprinkled with cinnamon.

SERVES 6

ALMOND AND CASHEW NUT COOKIES

1 cup (250 mL) shortening

1 cup (250 mL) white sugar

1 egg, beaten

3 tbsp (45 mL) ground almonds

3 tbsp (45 mL) ground cashew nuts

½ tsp (2.5 mL) vanilla extract

½ tsp (2.5 mL) almond extract

2½ cups (625 mL) all-purpose flour

1½ level tsp (7.5 mL) baking powder

pinch salt

1 Cream shortening and sugar together in a bowl. Add egg, almonds, cashews, vanilla and almond extract.

2 Sift flour, baking powder and salt together. Fold into creamed mixture and knead lightly. Shape dough into walnut-sized balls. Arrange on lightly greased baking sheets. Press each ball with a fork to flatten slightly.

3 Bake at 400°F (200°C) until pale golden, 15–20 minutes.

MAKES ABOUT 24

❖ **HINT**

When deep-frying food, only add small quantities of ingredients to the oil at one time. This maintains the oil's temperature and prevents oil absorption.

Almond and Cashew Nut Cookies

MEASURING MADE EASY

HOW TO MEASURE LIQUIDS

CUPS	U.S.	METRIC
2 tablespoons	1 fluid ounce	30 mL
¼ cup	2 fluid ounces	60 mL
	3 fluid ounces	90 mL
½ cup	4 fluid ounces	125 mL
	5 fluid ounces	150 mL
	5 1/2 fluid ounces	170 mL
¾ cup	6 fluid ounces	185 mL
	7 fluid ounces	220 mL
1 cup	8 fluid ounces	250 mL
2 cups	16 fluid ounces (1 pint)	500 mL
2½ cups	20 fluid ounces	625 mL
4 cups	32 fluid ounces (1 quart)	1 liter

HOW TO MEASURE DRY INGREDIENTS

½ oz		15 g
1 oz		30 g
2 oz		60 g
3 oz		90 g
4 oz	(¼ lb)	125 g
5 oz		155 g
6 oz		185 g
7 oz		220 g
8 oz	(½ lb)	250 g
9 oz		280 g
10 oz		315 g
11 oz		345 g
12 oz	(¾ lb)	375 g
13 oz		410 g
14 oz		440 g
15 oz		470 g
16 oz	(1 lb)	500 g
24 oz	(1½ lb)	750 g
32 oz	(2 lb)	1 kg

QUICK CONVERSIONS

¼ inch		5 mm
½ inch		1 cm
¾ inch		2 cm
1 inch		2.5 cm
2 inches		5 cm
2½ inches		6 cm
3¼ inches		8 cm
4 inches		10 cm
5 inches		12 cm
6 inches		15 cm
7 inches		18 cm
8 inches		20 cm
9 inches		22 cm
10 inches		25 cm
11 inches		28 cm
12 inches	(1 foot)	30 cm
18 inches		46 cm
20 inches		50 cm
24 inches	(2 feet)	61 cm
30 inches		77 cm

USING CUPS AND SPOONS

All cup and spoon measurements are level

¼ cup	2 fluid ounces	60 mL	¼ teaspoon	1.25 mL
⅓ cup	2½ fluid ounces	85 mL	½ teaspoon	2.5 mL
½ cup	4 fluid ounces	125 mL	1 teaspoon	5 mL
1 cup	8 fluid ounces	250 mL	1 tablespoon	15 mL

OVEN TEMPERATURES

FAHRENHEIT (°F)	CELSIUS (°C)	TEMPERATURES
250	120	Very slow
300	150	Slow
325-350	160-180	Moderately slow
375-400	190-200	Moderate
425-450	220-230	Moderately hot
475-500	250-260	Hot

INDEX